Praise for *Kids Ain't*

'Taking the very adult step of starting a family is oft
your money sorted it can turn one of life's most rewa.... ...g ...p......... .... something
incredibly stressful and much more difficult than it should be. *Kids Ain't Cheap* covers all
the key areas you need to get right to make the smartest money and investing moves for
your family (or future family).'

Ben Nash, financial adviser, founder of Pivot Wealth and author of
Replace Your Salary by Investing

'This book is a must-read for everyone who is a parent or planning to become a parent.
Ana goes through all the research, facts and things you need to know about before
having kids. Reading this book and applying some of the strategies Ana mentions
could save families thousands of dollars (and countless arguments later down the line)!
I highly recommend reading this book!'

Queenie Tan, Founder of Invest With Queenie

'Ana Kresina's *Kids Ain't Cheap* is the 'other' parenting book. This beautifully written
financial parenting book gives you a step-by-step guide to all things money and
parenting. Ana's book makes you see that you are not alone in navigating the costs of
raising your bundles of joy. Her stories, interviews, knowledge and facts make *Kids Ain't
Cheap* the only finance parenting book you'll ever need.'

Evan Lucas, author of *Mind over Money*, Head of Strategy at InvestSMART
and financial media personality

'Ana's detailed research and her own personal journey provide a roadmap for budgeting,
financial planning and investing while navigating the uncertainty of parental leave and
the often-overlooked costs of early childhood education and care (ouch). Recognising
the cultural inequities that influence financial literacy, Ana shares a wide range of
parenting experiences, emphasising the value of learning from one another.'

Molly Benjamin, founder of the Ladies Finance Club and author of
Girls Just Wanna Have Funds

'*Kids Ain't Cheap* comes at a critical point in time for those considering having children
in today's world. It is a meaningful resource for those of us who feel overwhelmed at
the prospect of affording children and empowers us with the tools we need to approach
potential parenthood with a plan.'

Emma Edwards, financial behaviour expert and founder of
The Broke Generation

'*Kids Ain't Cheap* is your roadmap to the most financially daunting – but rewarding –
experience in your life. So few books prepare families for the uncertainty of life's biggest
challenge, but *Kids Ain't Cheap* can help you navigate the complex and confusing world
of financial parenting.'

Owen Raszkiewicz, founder of Rask and host of the *Australian Finance Podcast*

KIDS AIN'T CHEAP

KIDS AIN'T CHEAP

How to plan financially for parenthood
and your family's future

ANA KRESINA

MAJOR
STREET

Acknowledgements

I acknowledge the Wurundjeri Woi Wurrung people as the traditional custodians of the land on which I live. From coast to coast, across land, waters and communities, I pay my respect to their Elders past, present and emerging.

To my parents, for supporting me in everything I do, hvala na svemu.

To Shawny bae, thank you for being my number one cheerleader.

To H & O, for bringing so much joy into my life, vi ste moja ljubav.

MAJOR STREET

First published in 2023 by Major Street Publishing Pty Ltd
info@majorstreet.com.au | +61 406 151 280 | majorstreet.com.au

A catalogue record for this book is available
from the National Library of Australia

Printed book ISBN: 978-1-922611-89-5
Ebook ISBN: 978-1-922611-90-1

Cover design by Tess McCabe
Internal design by Production Works
Printed in Australia by Griffin Press.

Thank you to Max Newnham CA – Financial Planning Specialist (Director TaxBiz Australia P/L) for consulting on this book.

10 9 8 7 6 5 4 3 2 1

Contents

Introduction

I never really thought about having kids when I was younger. In fact, it wasn't even a part of my future planning when I was in my 20s. For me, the ideal life consisted of travelling to exotic places, catching up with friends over brunch and trying new activities outside of my comfort zone. Nowhere in that equation was there room for children.

Then something crazy happened; I just changed my mind.

All of a sudden, I started thinking about how I wanted to have a family. I wanted to share my life with someone and fill it with love. I wanted something more than just enjoying life by myself.

I was single at the time, and I knew that parenthood would be an expensive undertaking. Not only were children expensive to raise, but taking parental leave would affect my career, earning potential and retirement savings – and that's not to mention any medical and fertility costs incurred prior to even conceiving. I figured if I wanted to start a family, I'd need to mentally and financially prepare to take this journey alone.

I immediately started focusing on reducing my expenses and increasing my income by advancing my career. In fact, I became determined to have a large financial safety net, as I wasn't exactly sure how much kids cost – I just knew they cost a lot!

Fast forward a few years (and a partner to boot). I was about five months pregnant with my first child and had just signed a contract to start a new position. That new position came with a pay increase, and I felt that I was doing all the right things financially in a general sense, but I was still unsure about all the unknowns of parenthood.

There's so much information on pregnancy and giving birth, but there's very little out there about navigating the financial side of things. The truth is that parents worry more about money in the lead up to having a baby than at any other time in their lives. There's a *massive* decrease in income and an increase in expenses. Plus, unlike when you use a budgeting app to figure out your monthly outgoings, kids don't come with a projected expense report.

With about 6 million families in Australia, and 300,000 babies born a year, I knew it couldn't just be me looking for support as I navigated one of the biggest transitions in life.

That is why I wrote *Kids Ain't Cheap*.

It is the resource I desperately wanted for myself. When I was expecting my first child, I needed to understand the financial impact of taking parental leave, what the superannuation gender gap means for me, how to budget for kids, the cost of early childhood education and care, and how to invest for my kids' futures. *Kids Ain't Cheap* is where those taking their first steps into the wonderful world of parenthood can find all that information and more.

In this book, you'll first learn how to think about money, work through budgeting for a family and explore all the costs associated with having a child. You'll also gain insight into what to expect on parental leave and how that can affect both your earning potential and your retirement savings. It's important to get these foundations right so that you feel empowered as you transition into your new role as parent.

You'll then jump into the often confusing (and unexpectedly expensive) world of early childhood education and care, gain the tools to choose the right centre and understand the requirements for any subsidies. These can be tricky to navigate, but you'll get the support you need to make educated choices for your family.

Finally, looking to the future, you'll learn the basics of investing and how to invest for your child so that you can give them a head start in life. By the end of the book, you'll also be equipped to teach your child about personal finance so that they can be confident in making their own financial decisions as they grow into adulthood.

As you can see, there's a lot to be covered in this book. It would be easy to feel overwhelmed by the sheer volume of things to think about when becoming a parent, but with *Kids Ain't Cheap* on hand, that's not going to happen to you. Each chapter concludes with actionable steps you can start taking immediately, with the express purpose of empowering you to start making financial decisions for your family's future today.

My perspective and yours

Before we begin, I want to note that this book was built on my own experience and that financial literacy is a privilege. When it comes to finances, so much inequality comes from systemic oppression, with the distribution of wealth affecting individuals differently, especially marginalised groups. Often, we are led to believe that poor financial outcomes are of our own making, when in reality, circumstance and education play significant roles in dictating financial literacy and the choices available to us.

Just having parents who talk about money can give someone a head start on their own financial journey. I was very fortunate to be raised by supportive parents who were able to teach me about saving and staying out of debt. Additionally, I'm a cisgender, straight-appearing, able-bodied white woman who was raised middle class, had access to education and now has a well-paid job. All of this is a privilege, and I would be doing us all a disservice to not acknowledge that this has affected my experiences and outcomes in life, especially when it comes to finances.

In this book, I've attempted to profile a diverse array of parents to share their stories and show how they are navigating the costs of parenthood. Everyone's journey is unique, and there is so much we can learn from others' experiences. I am grateful to all the parents who shared their journeys. These are my favourite parts of *Kids Ain't Cheap*.

As I researched this book, I was disappointed to find that most data represented and pertained to heteronormative family structures, with an emphasis on mothers being 'primary' caregivers. I've attempted to make this book as inclusive as possible, but with access to limited data in Australia, I recognise there's always room for improvement.

With the ever-changing landscape of government policies, schemes and subsidies, all of the information in this book was accurate at the time of writing. Please do your own research prior to making any financial decisions that may impact you or your family.

Lastly, thank you for taking the time to read this book. It was written between naps (both mine and my kids') during sleep-deprived parental leave with my second child. What motivated me to write *Kids Ain't Cheap* was the belief that if this resource had existed when I was just starting to plan for kids, I would have been able to make better financial decisions for my family. Hopefully it will help you as much as it would have helped me.

Chapter 1

Parenting money mindset

'Parenthood ... it's about guiding the next generation
and forgiving the last.'

Peter Krause

We all have money hang-ups. Our relationship with money is uniquely ours.

Whether we want to believe it or not, much of our understanding of money comes from our parents. In fact, a study from the University of Washington examined the financial decisions of twins and found that 33% of our financial behaviours can be attributed to genetics. That's not to say that other contributing factors don't affect our outlook on money; the contrary, they do as well.

During our childhood, much of our learning comes from social interactions, through which we learn the values, behaviours, norms and expectations of the world around us. As children we start to piece together our understanding of the value of money, work and the cost of items. A study by the University of Cambridge states that by age seven, our basic understanding of money – such as saving, budgeting and delayed gratification – is in place. There's no denying that most of this financial understanding comes from our parents; however, as we grow, the financial influence of our upbringing declines, while our parents' genetic influence proceeds throughout life.

Our lived experiences undoubtedly impact how we interact with our finances. Morgan Housel's book *The Psychology of Money* examines how different generations are impacted by the economic realities of their time. If times were tough and cash was hard to come by, your relationship to money was more likely one of scarcity, in which you believe you have limited resources and are more likely to be risk-averse. However, if you lived through a time that was plentiful, with lots of opportunity and very little economic downturn, it's likely you had more of an abundance mindset, in which your thinking around money is more positive and you are more likely to have a higher risk tolerance around money and business.

Of course, there are systemic issues we also need to consider when we examine our relationship with money. These include a lack of access to financial literacy, socioeconomic challenges, the gender gap, the racial wealth gap and discrimination against single parents and LGBTQIA+ families, all of which can increase the challenges of teaching healthy money habits and building generational wealth for families.

Over 3.3 million Australians live in poverty, which is one in eight people (including one in six children, and one in four people with disabilities), making it challenging to break the cycle. In fact, in Australia, with a history of colonisation, First Nations people have been denied access to wealth in the form of rights and freedoms, creating significant barriers, which only further impoverished communities based on systemic discrimination, impacting any chance of generational wealth in the form of knowledge or assets. This is just one example of how denying access to wealth in the form of property (which is one of the biggest accumulators of generational wealth) historically disadvantages groups of people through centuries of compounded inequality.

If you were fortunate enough to receive any financial literacy from your parents, that provided you with a privileged advantage. However, if you failed to receive that knowledge, at least you can break the cycle by passing on that information to your children now.

Although our relationship to money is deeply rooted in our genetics, relationships and understanding of the world, we can create positive habits and adjust our money mindset in order to set our families up for financial success.

How our money mindset affects our lives

Our experiences, beliefs and emotions about money directly affect our financial decisions. Even if we are extremely logical and have all the data in the world to make calculated decisions, we cannot help but be impacted by our own preconceived thoughts about money. This is often referred to as our 'money mindset'.

When I look back at my own parents' upbringing during times of poverty, immigration and recessions, it's clear that their experiences and understanding of the world around them impacted their relationship with money. Both my parents were very frugal, quite conservative when it came to financial risk and diligent about squirreling away any extra money for a rainy day. Many of the lessons I learned about money came from them. I often recall my father saying in an Eastern European accent, 'It's not how much you make but how much you save'. This statement really resonated with me through my formative years – as early as my first job I actively saved 10% of my paycheque – and continued into my adult years.

I learned from a young age that debt was bad and saving was good. However, I also heard such sentiments at the dinner table as 'investing is gambling', which always made me wary about the stock market. It's only in my 30s that I actively became interested in building wealth and educated myself about investing in order to change my understanding of something I inherently believed was true. To understand my own money mindset and psychology, I really needed to dig deep into understanding why I thought the way I did.

Reflecting on how our families talk about money and how we feel about money is important as it gives insight into our own beliefs. More importantly, it gives us the ability to reflect and decide which of those beliefs we want to hold onto and which we want to let go of.

If our parents deeply affected our own understanding of money, surely we will do the same to our children. So, doesn't it make sense to examine our own relationships with money? In doing so, we can drop any limiting beliefs that don't serve us and take on new, empowering beliefs that we can pass on to our children.

Ultimately, we want to build a secure future for our children, but that first begins with us as parents.

Limiting money beliefs

Limiting beliefs are attitudes, emotions and behaviours that hold us back from making positive changes to improve our financial situation.

To reflect on your own money psychology, ask yourself if there's anything you've previously believed to be true that can be limiting your mindset. Here are some examples:

- Money is the root of all evil.
- Managing money is too stressful.
- I'll never have enough money to be happy.
- My net worth equals my self-worth.
- I'm bad at maths, so I'll never be good at money.
- I deserve to spend money on myself whenever I feel like it.
- I don't deserve to ever treat myself.
- If I had more money I'd be able to manage my money better.
- Talking about money is taboo.

Once you identify your limiting beliefs, you need to understand your reasons for supporting them and begin to reframe your understanding of them. This will then rewire your thinking in order to create new empowering beliefs that will support you.

Here are some steps to overcome these limiting beliefs:

1. **Identify the limiting belief.** What is the belief that you hold? Where did it come from? Why do you believe it to be true?

2. **Reframe your belief so it is empowering.** How can you reframe your limiting belief to be supportive of your new thoughts? What affirmations can you use to help you believe your new, empowered belief? By affirming your new belief, you are effectively rewiring your brain, enabling you to create new mental pathways that align with your new way of thinking.

3. **Build new habits to support your empowered belief.** What are some active steps you can take to support your new belief? How can you use language that positively supports your new belief? By actively creating new habits and using language to support your belief, you are reinforcing your new ideology as true to you, which can be empowering.

Here's an example of a limiting belief of mine: I believed that I wasn't smart enough to start investing. I thought it was too hard and complicated and only reserved for stockbrokers who have millions of dollars to play with. Plus, as I mentioned earlier, I believed it was very risky and another form of gambling (thanks to my parents).

As I started to question why I felt this way, I realised that it was because of how society portrayed investing – using complex jargon and terms to make me feel stupid. Plus, because there was very little female representation when it came to investing, I just didn't think I could do it.

Once I identified my belief and reframed it as a belief that I *could* in fact learn to invest, I supported my new, empowered belief by starting to teach myself about investing. I devoured books and blogs on the topic and was delighted to learn that women are, in fact, better investors than men and take fewer risks when investing. This new belief became my truth and helped me overcome any negative self-talk I had about not being smart enough. If I can rewire my thinking about money, surely anyone can!

Money can buy happiness

Another common limiting belief is that money can't buy happiness. In a 2022 study on poverty reduction intervention, evidence showed that providing mothers experiencing poverty unconditional cash payments may improve brain development in babies. When considering the socioeconomic challenges that low-income earners face, money *can* buy happiness, but more so, it can set your child up for better future outcomes and development. Of course, happiness is derived from the things we love: spending time with our friends and family, and having the freedom to explore our interests and be stress-free. The reality is that even though those things bring happiness, the lack of money can bring on a lot of financial stress that can detract from those moments.

A 2023 study re-examined the dominant thought that money made people happier only until their incomes hit US$75,000 (AU$109,155 at the time of writing), at which point their happiness plateaued. The original research from 2021 affirmed the belief that money doesn't buy happiness. However, when the researchers relooked at their findings, they found that emotional wellbeing continues to rise well beyond US$200,000 (AU$291,080 at the time of writing). The 20% of participants that were the *least* happy were those whose level of joy didn't rise with their income. Essentially, if you're a happy person, an increase in income will continue to provide happiness, and if you're an unhappy person, no amount of money will make you happy.

So, why is this important?

As a parent, you are the anchor for your family and children; your wellbeing is paramount to their development and sense of security. Having financial security will reduce your stress, provide more happiness (if you're not a grump to begin with!) and create a more plentiful future for your family.

All of this begins with you.

Focus on what you can control

Parenting can be stressful. There's a lot to consider, such as balancing money, time and sleep. Luckily, there are things we can control, such as offering our kids delicious, home-cooked meals – but that doesn't mean they'll be eaten. I always feel so sad when my perfectly plated dish gets pushed aside by my toddler or swung halfway across the kitchen by my baby. We can lead a child to broccoli, but we can't force them to eat it. The positive thing is that we did what was within our control by providing them with healthy food. That which isn't in our circle of control – getting them to eat it – we sometimes need to stress about a tad less.

Finances are very similar. Money can be stressful; in fact, 47% of Australians experience some form of financial stress and 51% worry about paying monthly expenses. Inflation, interest rates, share market fluctuation and housing prices – Australia's favourite topic – all affect our everyday lives. However, none of them are things that we can directly control. We can't reduce inflation or interest rates, and we absolutely can't manipulate the share market (unless you have a huge amount of pull on social media… but that's a topic for another day). As for housing, wouldn't it be lovely if prices dropped when you were looking to buy and skyrocketed when you were hoping to sell? Regardless, if we can't control these things, why stress about them?

Stress and worry come from the desire to have control over a situation. However, if we try to control things that we can't impact, we just become more anxious and stressed. It's a vicious cycle to break out of. We worry, then we try to control, but we can't control, so we feel more helpless and stressed, so we try to control things again. The cycle repeats.

There are a few things you can do to break the cycle and focus on your own wellbeing and what's within your circle of control and concern. The circle of control and concern is simple. The circle of concern contains all the things that worry you but that you can't do anything about, such as inflation and interest rates, or the cost of early childhood education and care (ECEC). Within that circle is a smaller circle, the circle of control, which contains all the things you can control with your thoughts and actions, such as money habits, your ability to reduce expenses or increase your income, choosing the right school for your kid and choosing how much parental leave you take (see figure 1.1).

Figure 1.1: the circle of control and concern

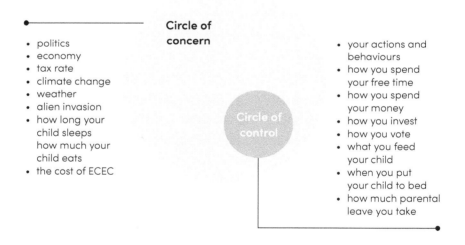

Circle of concern

- politics
- economy
- tax rate
- climate change
- weather
- alien invasion
- how long your child sleeps
  how much your child eats
- the cost of ECEC

Circle of control

- your actions and behaviours
- how you spend your free time
- how you spend your money
- how you invest
- how you vote
- what you feed your child
- when you put your child to bed
- how much parental leave you take

If we identify the things we have control over and focus less on the things we can't control, we can train our brains to diffuse stress and create impactful change. By asking, 'Is this something I can directly impact or change?' we are able to focus on the things we can control and how we deal with them.

Now, the truth is that worrying happens regardless. I know there have been some late nights when I've lain in bed thinking about random stressors. I've found that getting up and writing them all down helps. In fact, scheduling time for stress is helpful. Studies have shown that allocating time to worry can reduce anxiety and insomnia. Whether it's a 30-minute session of uninterrupted gloom-and-doom thinking or a quick note-taking session, reducing anxiety about that which you can't control can help you focus on that which is within your control – like parenting and your finances.

Building good financial habits

Creating good financial habits is well within your control. In fact, I want you to say this out loud:

I am good with money.
I am financially savvy.
I am an investor.

Do you believe those sentiments? You should! It's your new identity. You are a financially savvy investor who is great with money! From now on, as you move forward, this is your mantra and something you will take on as your identity.

James Clear's book *Atomic Habits* looks at small changes we make in our lives and how they can have a compounding effect. Just imagine the effects of improving by 1% every day. It can be huge (see figure 1.2 overleaf)! He identifies three main behavioural changes: goal-driven, system-driven and identity-driven, with the third being the most impactful for long-lasting change.

If we begin to believe we are financially savvy investors, we will start to think and act like financially savvy investors. Creating a new identity for ourselves allows us to create habits that support that new belief. By changing the core belief, you may even trigger a chain reaction of other beliefs.

Figure 1.2: 1% better every day

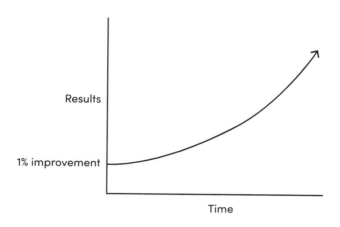

SOURCE: *ATOMIC HABITS*, JAMES CLEAR

Would a financially savvy investor save money for a holiday or go into debt to travel? Would a financially savvy investor negotiate a lower mortgage rate or avoid a phone call to the bank? Would a financially savvy investor start putting away $5 a month for their child's investment account or avoid investing altogether?

I think we all know what a financially savvy investor would do – because it's what you would do! You are a financially savvy investor! (If you don't like the term 'financially savvy investor', come up with your own: 'fantastic frugal father', 'money manic mama', 'the wealth generator'… the point is, you need to resonate with the new identity and take it on as your own.)

With your new identity, it's easier to set goals and have systems in place to achieve them. It's actually easiest to achieve your goals by setting good habits. Clear states that by improving a behaviour by 1%, over time that improvement compounds and can lead to a significant transformation.

Let's say you start identifying as someone who is athletic. You believe you are athletic, and therefore you decide to go to the gym a minimum of three times a week. You won't get abs immediately (actually, you may never get abs), but over time you will start to feel healthier and fitter. You may even want to eat healthier due to the changes you feel in your body. Perhaps you even save more money because you are less likely to drink alcohol. Maybe you even join a sports team, increasing your social time and dopamine levels. The effects of a small change can have a massive impact, and this all stemmed from your new belief.

Similarly, if you believe you are a financially savvy investor, you will start to think like one. It's also easier to then take up the other habit approaches Clear shares in his book – the first being goal-driven, which may be something like wanting to invest $10,000 in your child's investment account. Since you have a goal in mind, you will work towards it, depositing money into the investment account each payday. Or you may focus on having more financially streamlined systems like automating your child's investments, so that you remove the mental load of thinking about it but are still contributing, which Clear identifies as a system-driven habit. By making habits as low-friction as possible, you'll be more likely to follow through and create longer-lasting habits.

The point is that there are different ways to create habits that support building a better financial future for you and your family. Whether they are goal-driven, system-driven or identity-driven, small, incremental changes can have a profound effect. Even the small act of saving $100 can turn into $1,000,000 in 40 years (which we will talk about in chapter 7), all due to the power of having good financial habits.

So, let's talk about the financial things you can control, such as getting your finances in order before having kids, which we will talk about in the next chapter.

Actionable steps

- Reflect on how your parents' money mindset affected your own relationship with money. This can be positive or negative.

- Write down some of the money beliefs that you grew up with. Are these money beliefs that you still hold today?

- Write down any limiting money beliefs that you have and reframe them into a new belief. Take a moment to sit with them and take on the identity of the new belief.

- Create a new money identity that you connect with and begin to embody that new label. Whether it be 'financially savvy investor' or otherwise, take steps to believe that this is your new identity, including any new habits to solidify this belief.

- Write down all the items that are within your circle of control and concern. If you can identify items you wish to change that are within your control, take actionable steps on adjusting them as needed.

Lauren

33 | husband Jarrad (34), twins Hugo and Hudson (3) | Adelaide Hills, SA

What was your upbringing around money?

I was a good saver because I saw my mum struggle with money. Since my dad was a gambler, we were a single-mum household, and I can vividly remember my mum asking, 'Can I just borrow $50 out of your money box, and I'll replace it on Thursday?' Thursday was payday, so she was getting through that fortnight to put food on the table. Not realising at the time that I took that all in, I've gone the complete opposite – if anything, I've hoarded money, so I've had to work on that.

How did you prepare yourself financially for parenthood?

The main financial factor that we thought about was how to maximise my maternity leave. I actually took half-pay maternity leave from my job to extend it and then took the Centrelink Parental Leave Pay over the Christmas break when my maternity leave finished.

It wasn't until the twins were born that we got clear on our budget and tracked expenses to ensure we could work within my maternity-leave entitlements. We were also preparing for me to return to work in a part-time capacity (12 months after the twins were born) and had to ensure we could live off the reduced earnings and cover the childcare costs, which are substantial. I did all the calculations to determine the best option for childcare and returning to work part time. That is how we settled on three days a week.

What was the biggest financial challenge you needed to navigate?

We did purchase a house knowing we were very early on in our pregnancy, but we didn't know we were having twins. If we had known, we possibly would have purchased a slightly larger house. However, with the current climate of interest rates, I am very glad we didn't. I also believe if I knew we were going to have twins we would have put more effort into saving beforehand. We were in good money routines, but we definitely could have been more strategic.

How has having twins impacted your finances?

My husband often joked about saving on inflation by having two babies at once. With the way the economy is at the moment, maybe we actually did! However, buying two of absolutely everything put a dent in our finances.

The biggest expense overall has been childcare. Currently it is approximately $19,500 a year for the two of them (three days a week). When they were younger it was more, but further subsidies have come in, making it cheaper. This is a nice reprieve for us, considering the cost of living at the moment.

The Australian government doesn't consider twins as a multiple birth when it comes to subsidies. How did this impact your family?

I can tell you right now that I had more than one baby. However, I do also understand where the government is coming from. Twins are much more common than triplets or higher-order multiples and, therefore, having subsidies for twins would require a huge increase in monetary support from the government, and where would this money come from?

I know multiple birth associations support and help where they can with discounted formula, et cetera. I feel fortunate that we were financially stable before we had twins and could continue to stay that way. However, I do worry about families that are not in our position.

What are some of the things you've done to increase your income?

I have always been one to go all in with whatever it is I am doing. Teaching used to solely be my job until my partner (now husband) stated I needed a hobby. Hobbies from there have included blogging, candle making and jewellery making. Businesses have grown out of my blogging, where I make money from advertising and affiliate marketing.

I now also have a business as a financial coach supporting mums and women with their finances and to bring in additional income. I did this because I knew if we as a family wanted to see the world while also having the option to live life on our terms and not within the nine-to-five, we needed to increase our incomes.

How has having children changed your family's financial goals?

We are now a lot more serious about our personal finance goals. We are much more future-focused and have started investing to ensure we hit our main goal of being financially free as soon as possible while still enjoying life. Sacrifices have definitely needed to be made. We prioritise investing via salary sacrifice and direct investing as well as putting money aside for family holidays. Ideally, I want to be able to live overseas and travel with my family.

Have you done any estate or life planning?

We have, 100%. Having the twins was the instigator for this. We have since completed our wills, advance care directives and powers of attorney. We have also had our insurances looked at by a financial adviser. Having completed all of this brings great peace of mind knowing that our children will be looked after if something horrible were to happen.

Do you have any advice for anyone planning on having kids?

You will be overwhelmed with the amount of advice out there when it comes to parenting. You will be given one piece of advice from one person and the complete opposite from someone else. Therefore, my best piece of advice would be to trust your gut.

Alex

44 | partner (37), three kids (13, 11 and 2) | Melbourne, Vic.

What was your upbringing around money?

Middle class, I guess. We owned our own home, two kids in private schools. Money was never discussed, nor did we appear to have financial issues growing up.

How did you prepare financially for parenthood?

I did no preparation at all for my first two kids. I was the sole breadwinner and money was extremely tight. With my second child we saved money so that my partner could have more time at home before returning to work.

Do you and your partner have a similar money mindset?

No, not initially, but we have grown together around making financial decisions. I have become more conscious about how I spend money. My partner spends less money on food than I did initially. I would buy organic whole foods even if I couldn't realistically afford it for the kids, but now I'm more relaxed about the quality of food.

What are your family's biggest financial challenges?

We recently paid off our mortgage, which would have been our greatest financial pressure. We were only able to do this thanks to an inheritance I received. Other than that, it is private school fees, childcare, groceries and then utilities.

How did you navigate separation when it came to finances?

When I separated from my previous partner, I agreed to cover rent and living expenses for the kids, which was more than I could afford, but I wanted to keep things the same for the kids. The only assets we had were a car and household items, which I gave to my ex-partner. I paid these living expenses for roughly 12 months and then paid a reduced amount; however, this was still higher than what was required by child support. This was negotiated using some mediation, but mostly agreed between me and my ex-partner.

How has having children changed your family's financial goals and lifestyle?

I don't think my goals have changed, but lifestyle has changed, including eating out less, going on holidays less, spending less money on personal items for myself (such as clothing). I'm not really someone who has had big personal goals financially.

How are you thinking about generational wealth for your kids?

I'm not. However, we just did our will and spilt the assets between the three kids.

How are you teaching your children about money and finances?

We try to educate our kids about the problems of credit and loans, as well as impulsive buying and gambling. As my kids have ADHD (attention deficit hyperactivity disorder) I have concerns for their future money management, so I talk to them a lot about the costs of things.

My son got a job at 12 years of age (a $30 per week paper round) so that he could begin to learn about money management, which has helped him to understand the problems with in-game purchasing and so on. He is able to save up for things he wants, and he likes the autonomy of having his own money. I think kids getting jobs early is key to them learning about money management.

My kids also have a copy of *Barefoot Kids* by Scott Pape.

Is there anything you wish you knew prior to having kids?

Not really. I think I knew what I needed to know. However, I have two kids with disabilities and I did not expect the additional costs associated with allied health (speech pathology, paediatricians, occupational therapy) and the kids having to attend private schools due to their needs being higher than expected.

Do you have any advice for new parents?

There is no right time to have kids. Don't leave it too late as it gets harder physically and emotionally the older you are. Also have no expectations of your kids.

What was the best piece of advice you've received regarding parenthood?

'Good enough' parenting.

Chapter 2

Getting your finances in order before kids

'Making the decision to have a child is momentous.
It is to decide forever to have your heart go walking
around outside your body.'

Elizabeth Stone

You may have known you wanted kids your whole life, or perhaps, like me, you realised you wanted them at age 30 when your ovaries started kicking into overdrive and made you swoon over every baby you saw. (WTF? That was the weirdest turn of events as I finished my third decade on earth.)

Either way, kids ain't cheap, so preparing ahead of time is key to reducing any financial stress that comes with them.

In Australia, 41% of households comprise a couple with children, and since money issues are one of the leading causes of divorce, with 20% to 40% of divorces being attributed to financial problems (not to mention the negative impact parenthood has on romantic relationships, but that's a topic for another time), now may be as good a time as any to consider your family's future. If you're a single parent or carer (which is about 11% to 12% of households), it's even more crucial to be aware of your finances, seeing as single-parent households have lower average financial wellbeing and you're the sole breadwinner.

The 2021 census recorded 78,425 same-sex couples, 17% of whom have children. Although same-sex couples have higher incomes than different-sex couples on average, LGBTQIA+ families may need to consider additional costs when it comes to family planning and fertility. Regardless of your family situation, being prepared financially will provide you with security so you can focus on more important things, like your little ones.

Before we get into the planning of parental leave and the costs of having kids, we need to ensure that your financial health is on track, so let's get started.

The importance of reducing stress by preparing yourself financially

There are so many delightful moments in parenthood: that toothy grin, the big wet kisses, or even when they whisper 'I love you' in your ear for the first time. Those moments are pure magic.

But the counterpart to that is that kids are exhausting: the poo explosions, the sleepless nights, the defiant toddler years (I'm a firm believer that age three is worse than two). There's also the reality of post-partum depression – which 40% of Australian women experience and which can affect both parents – making the first few months of parenthood challenging and, if you're partnered, possibly putting a strain on your relationship.

In fact, psychotherapist and marriage researcher John Gottman studied couples who transitioned into parenthood and discovered that 67% experienced a decline in relationship satisfaction in the first three years of their baby's life. He also found in the study that most couples that break up within the first seven years of marriage do so because they became parents. His research states that all couples – straight or gay – have the same challenges, but that same-sex couples are more likely to use humour and the ability to calm down to help them persevere through hard times.

Similarly, a study by Nobel prize–winning psychologist Daniel Kahneman shows that working women rank taking care of children as one of the least enjoyable activities, barely above commuting, working and housework (and to be honest, cleaning the bathroom is also one of my least favourite chores). In fact, another study suggests that even if there are support systems in place and financial stability, overall parents are less happy than their childless counterparts.

So, what are the resounding findings of these studies? Parenthood can make you quite unhappy and finances are a leading cause of stress among couples. Therefore, if there's any financial conflict in your current life, there is a good chance that it will be exacerbated by having kids.

Now, by no means am I suggesting that having kids will make you miserable (despite studies suggesting otherwise). However, it may be useful to consider how to set yourself up for a smooth transition to parenthood by reducing stress. And since money can be one of the leading causes of stress, what better way to do this than to get your finances in order?

Track your spending, debt and net worth

One of the first steps to getting your finances in order is to track your spending.

The benefit of this is to gain a better understanding of your spending habits. That way you know exactly what wiggle room you have between your income and expenses and how much of that you can save, invest or spend, depending on your goals. By monitoring your spending, you can see which areas you are overpaying in (such as utilities), which need a buffer (possibly the savings account) and where you can cut costs (ahem, streaming subscriptions).

The goal is to increase your financial stability in the event of an emergency or unforeseen cost. Plus, it's advantageous to know how much additional money you have in case extra expenses are incurred when you have a bub.

The best way to start is to calculate your income. Just add up your annual wage and any additional money you receive (such as from a side hustle, rental money or dividends). Often this is a fixed amount, unless you run a business or actively hustle to increase your income.

It's far more challenging to calculate exactly what your monthly expenses are or what you spend annually. By listing all the items you spend money on, you can have an understanding of where you spend your money and how much you spend. There are tons of free apps you can use that link directly to your bank account and allow you to filter and label your costs. These apps are great for setting up budgets and ensuring you are adhering to your spending limits. Plus, it can be quite illuminating to see how many times you ordered Uber Eats over the last month. When using an app like this, double-check that it is covered under open banking, which is accredited by the Australian Competition and Consumer Commission (ACCC), meaning that the banks have the right to share your data with these apps in a safe and regulated way (but don't worry, they can't use your banking information to make purchases).

If you're more the manual type and don't like apps, download a budgeting spreadsheet to help you stay accountable. Sometimes the manual process of documenting your purchases can motivate you to spend less.

Whatever you choose, understanding where your money goes monthly is a great way to stay on top of your finances.

Know your net worth

Working in the technology sector, we often say, 'You can't improve what you don't measure', so the first step in increasing your net worth is to track it. Similarly, tracking your net worth can empower you to increase your savings, decrease your debt and stay the course of achieving financial security.

To calculate your net worth, add up all your assets: cash, investments, property and so on. Then, subtract all your liabilities, such as your mortgage, HECS-HELP debt and any credit card debt you may have. The resulting number is your net worth.

Personally, I find it motivating to track my net worth monthly and see it increase over time while my debt decreases, showing me how far I've come. Even if your net worth is low or in the negatives, know that by taking these first steps in tracking your finances you are already making a positive change to your relationship with money.

Budgeting your expenses

Ugh, budgeting. Everyone hates that word. I know I do. But honestly, budgeting doesn't have to be scary. It can be as simple as allocating a set amount of money for expenses each month and saving or investing the rest. Or it can consist of setting up categories in an app, or using the bucket method (popularised by *The Barefoot Investor*), which allocates a percentage of your income to your needs, wants, emergency fund and future self.

The benefit is that you can hold yourself accountable and see if there are any financial anomalies in your spending. Plus, it's pretty illuminating to see that you're actually spending $500 on eating out instead of the $200 you've budgeted. Ultimately, if you can increase the gap between your income and your expenses, then you will have money to prepare for the bottomless pit of costs known as children.

There is a ton of different budgeting methods, so find one that works for you. The goal is not to feel overwhelmed by the process but to keep yourself financially accountable.

Once you have an idea of how much you spend monthly, especially on necessities, you can then figure out how much money you need for other goals, such as travel, a deposit for a house or even simple splurge items like going out for a nice celebratory dinner. This will also allow you to determine how much money you can allocate to child expenses, including early childhood education and care (ECEC) costs (provided you send your kid to ECEC).

Now, this isn't a budgeting book per se, but it is important to ensure you can weather any storms as your expenses increase with the addition of a little human, whether that be loss of job, health issues or a car breakdown. Having a budget – knowing about and being more aware of your money – can keep you on track.

Splitting expenses with a partner

If you're coupled, the conversation around joining finances and splitting expenses is important to have, especially prior to having a child. Every relationship is different, and personal finance is… well, personal. So, figure out what works best for your relationship situation.

If you're single, this section may not be relevant, but it may be valuable to consider if you choose to enter a relationship in the future.

There are various options in splitting expenses within a couple. They are:

- 50/50 split of expenses
- equitable savings percentage
- combining finances.

Let's dive deeper into the options.

A very common way to divide expenses with a partner is a **50/50 split of expenses** (see table 2.1). Rent, utilities and food are all split in half. This does not take anyone's income or desired savings into consideration.

This option can allow for autonomy as only the joint expenses are divided, allowing each individual to do their own spending, saving and investing. It can provide security for each person as they can decide how to budget and allocate their income to other things. This also works well if two people don't share similar goals when it comes to money. The downside is that if one person is a high-income earner, this system can create a disparity in savings and cause financial stress for the lower income earner. For example, in a partnership where expenses are $3000 a month, the couple would split the expenses equally, resulting in each person paying $1500.

Table 2.1: sharing expenses 50/50 regardless of income

	Person 1	Person 2
Income	$8000/month	$4000/month
Expenses paid %	50%	50%
Expenses paid $	$1500	$1500
Monthly savings $	$6500	$2500
Monthly savings %	81.3%	62.5%

Some couples want to ensure that both partners have a more **equitable savings percentage** at the end of the month and that their expenses are divided accordingly (see table 2.2). This option is great for those who want to ensure that both people can save, invest and spend equitably regardless of their income. This ensures that the lower income earner pays a lower percentage of the expense, but an equal percentage of their income in relation to the other person. This is one of the most equitable ways to split expenses and have financial autonomy.

Table 2.2: ensuring that the percentage of savings is equally distributed

	Person 1	Person 2
Income	$8000/month	$4000/month
Expenses paid %	66.6%	33.3%
Expenses paid $	$2000	$1000
Monthly savings $	$6000	$3000
Monthly savings %	75%	75%

This is calculated by taking the overall income, then calculating each person's income as a percentage of the total. In the example set out in table 2.2, the total income is $12,000 a month, and each partner's contribution to that total is 66.6% (100 / 12000 × 8000 = 66.6%) and 33.3% (100 / 12000 × 4000 = 33.3%). The overall expenses, which come to $3000 in total, are then divided by each person's percentage of the total income, equalling $2000 (3000 × 66.6% = 2000) and $1000 (3000 × 33.3% = 1000) respectively. To verify that savings are equally distributed in relation to the total income, divide 100 by the person's income and then multiplying by their remaining income. This will give you the percentage of the person's income that can be saved each month. For person 1 in this example, that looks like this: 100 / 8000 × 6000 = 75%. For person 2: 100 / 4000 × 3000 = 75%.

For those who want to pool all their money, **combining finances** is great for those who share both their expenses and savings in one account regardless of income earned by either partner (see table 2.3). This is a common option for couples who are married, have lived together for a long period of time, or own assets together. The benefit is shared and transparent finances, but the downside can be disagreements on how the money should be used.

Table 2.3: equally sharing expenses and savings in one account regardless of income

	Person 1 and person 2
Income	$12,000/month
Expenses paid %	100%
Expenses paid $	$3000
Monthly savings $	$9000
Monthly savings %	75%

Dividing expenses with a partner is highly personal, and I've used many of these options. In fact, my partner and I had separate finances even after our first child was born (we used the first two options). We only opted to combine our finances after we purchased our home with our second baby on the way (option three).

There's no right or wrong way to split expenses with a partner, but it is valuable to consider what works best in your situation.

Your emergency fund

A while back, I was planning on freezing my eggs. I had a budget for the massive expense, but when I saw the fertility specialist, I discovered that I had very bad endometriosis that had taken over my fallopian tubes and my right ovary. In order to move forward with the egg extraction and increase my chances of fertility in the future, I needed to get a laparoscopic surgery. Due to the timeline, I needed to act fast on this surgery, and since the waitlist for the public system was over a year, I was grateful to have an emergency fund that I could use.

An emergency fund isn't for everyday expenses or splurges – it's for unforeseen expenses that are literally... well, an emergency. An example is loss of income, such as if you lose your job or have a healthcare issue, or your home floods. Ideally, an emergency fund should contain about three to six months' worth of expenses. For those caregivers who plan on taking an extended period of leave from work, your emergency fund may be even larger – up to 12 months' worth of expenses. It all depends on your risk tolerance, how many income streams you have and how comfortable you want to be once taking leave. Other things to consider include your relationship status and if you're eligible to receive any parental leave payment from the government or your workplace.

As a single parent, it's crucial to have an emergency fund and savings in case complications arise and you need to take a longer time off work or pay for postnatal treatment. An emergency fund is a safety net that ensures you can weather the storm if something unexpected happens. It can also provide you with peace of mind as you navigate parenthood, knowing you have money set aside if needed.

Paying off your consumer debt

If you're starting a family, one of the biggest financial hurdles worth overcoming is consumer debt. Consumer debts are personal debts that are used to purchase depreciating assets (items that don't go up in value over time) for household consumption. They include credit card debt, student loans and Buy Now Pay Later debt.

There are many reasons why someone may have consumer debt, including having to fund leaving a toxic job, dependency on debt when going through a divorce, or just a lack of financial literacy. (Remember, the system is set up for us to not be successful at money management.) And let's be honest, with the introduction of Buy Now Pay Later products and, of course, credit cards, it's never been easier to rack up debt.

Consumer debt can be very debilitating when it comes to building wealth, so it's advantageous to tackle it as soon as you have an emergency fund set up. If you do have a large amount of consumer debt, it's best to pay off as much as you can prior to having children. If you already have kids, it's smart to prioritise paying it off as soon as possible. The longer it takes to pay off the debt, the more interest you end up paying, meaning you will ultimately spend more money than the original debt amount due to the accrued interest over time. We talk more about debt and how to talk to your kids about it in chapter 8.

There are two main strategies to pay off debt. The first is the **avalanche method**. This method saves you the most amount of money by focusing on the highest-interest debts first. Basically, you order all your debts from highest interest to lowest. Then you focus on paying off the highest-interest debt while making the minimum repayments on all your other debts. The goal is to pay off the highest-interest debt as quickly as you can, which can result in paying less interest than if you tried to pay off all the debts equally.

The second strategy is called the **snowball method**, and it can be a huge motivator for anyone trying to overcome debt. The goal is to pay off the lowest balance of debt first. Once that is paid off, you move on to the second-lowest amount. Unfortunately, when doing the maths, this will most likely end up costing you more in interest rates in the long run compared with the first strategy. However, it can be a huge motivator to pay off debt quickly by focusing on small wins along the way.

The point of both strategies is to get you out of the red, so it doesn't matter which method you choose – if it gets you out of debt then the strategy is working. This will then free up additional cash flow for your family's financial goals.

Investing

What I love about investing is that your money makes money. Through the power of compound interest, you can build wealth and generate a passive income that builds security for you and your family.

I won't dive deep into investing at this point because I've dedicated a whole chapter to understanding investing (see chapter 6) and another to investing for your child (see chapter 7). But it is worth mentioning that if you are in good financial standing and have some extra cash that you won't need to access for at least seven years, investing may be a good option to consider to build wealth for your family's future.

Automating your money

If the main goal of getting your finances in order is to create security and opportunity for your family's future, the second goal may be to have more time on your hands. Time is everything when you have demanding little humans and barely have a moment to brush your teeth. A good way to free up some time is to automate your finances.

Some ways you can do this include ensuring direct-debit bill payments happen on time and depositing a set amount into your emergency fund each payday. If you are building wealth through investing (see chapter 6) automating your investments is a great way to guarantee you are investing at regular intervals (also known as dollar cost averaging).

By automating your finances, you are ensuring that each bill is paid, money is set aside for your savings goals and you're able to invest for your family and future self. Plus, it frees up your mental load so you can focus on more important things, such as ordering cupcakes for baby's first birthday party.

Boosting your retirement fund

Super is a great tax savings vehicle that can help fund your retirement. However, in 2020, $13.8 billion was held as lost or unclaimed superannuation across Australia. It's no wonder super goes missing when people change jobs on average every three years and their new companies suggest they sign up to the company's nominated super fund. One of the best things you can do to ensure your super is working for you is to find any lost super and consolidate it, and the Australian Taxation Office (ATO) has a great tool to help you do so.

At time of writing, your employer is required to pay 11% of your wage into super (it's set to rise to 12% by July 2025). Retirement may seem so far away that it feels silly to be thinking about super when parenthood is the more immediate money concern, but if you do have any additional wiggle room, it may be worth considering salary-sacrificing (pre-tax) contributions into your super, especially if you are in a high tax bracket. One benefit is that it can be used for the First Home Super Saver (FHSS) scheme, which allows you to save money for your first home inside your super fund, but it can also help reduce the super gender gap that you or your partner may encounter by taking parental leave. The truth is that women earn $1.01 million less than men on average during their working lives and end up with $136,000 less in super at retirement. Also, with women over 55 being one of the most vulnerable groups to homelessness and poverty, it's important for women to consider their super.

Therefore, if you have any spare change to boost your super prior to having children, this may be the time to do it. The Association of Superannuation Funds of Australia (ASFA) estimates how much money you'll need in retirement, depending on your lifestyle (see table 2.4). Keep in mind, though, that this is based on people who have paid off their homes by retirement.

Table 2.4: how much money you'll need to retire at age 67

ASFA retirement standard	Annual living costs	Weekly living costs	Savings required
Single – modest	$31,785	$611	$100,000
Couple – modest	$45,808	$880	$100,000
Single – comfortable	$50,004	$961	$595,000
Couple – comfortable	$70,482	$1355	$690,000

All figures in today's dollars using 2.75% average weekly earnings as a deflator and an assumed investment earning rate of 6 per cent. The fact that the same savings are required for a modest retirement for both couples and singles reflects the impact of receiving the age pension.

SOURCE: ASFA

At the very least, it's worth tracking if you are on par to accumulate the national average for super at retirement (see table 2.5).

We will dive deeper into the super gender gap and what you can do to increase your super for retirement in chapter 4.

Table 2.5: average super balances by age compared with
ASFA's comfortable retirement benchmark

Age	ASFA comfortable retirement benchmark by end of age range	Average balance (men)	Average balance (women)
15–24	$17,000	$6500	$5100
25–34	$93,000	$42,100	$34,500
35–44	$195,000	$107,700	$76,900
45–54	$330,000	$219,300	$136,000
55–64	$415,000	$326,200	$246,300

SOURCE: ASFA AND ABS

Increasing your income

There's always a limit to how much you can reduce your expenses. Cutting lattes and forgoing buying new shoes only takes you so far. On the other hand, there's no ceiling to how much you can earn. The biggest investment you can make in life is in yourself – upskilling and increasing your earning potential will take you far further than any little savings hacks ever will.

If you already have a baby on the way, it may be hard to increase your income with only a few months to go, but there are a few low-effort things you might be able to do. You could start a small side hustle, sell some unused items on marketplace or even ask for a wage increase prior to taking parental leave. (Tell your employer this is a great incentive to return to work.)

There's a growing percentage of parents, especially mothers, starting side hustles and businesses while caring for their children. The flexibility, opportunity and income allow parents to work from home while balancing their career and parenting duties. This option may not be for everyone, but the truth is that increasing your income can provide security and alleviate stress for you and your family.

Joining the FIRE movement

If you've nailed all your finances and are looking for the next step, it may be worth looking into the Financial Independence, Retire Early (FIRE) movement. The FIRE movement, popularised by Mr. Money Mustache, focuses on saving aggressively and investing any spare dollars in order to live off passive income from investments. Those striving for financial independence and the ability to choose their own opportunities may want to consider this ideology.

A famous study often referred to as the 'Trinity study' suggests that if you have 25 times your annual expenses invested, you'd be able to live indefinitely off that amount. For example, if your annual expenses are $40,000, you would want to have $1 million invested (because 40,000 × 25 = 1,000,000). Achieving this does require a fairly high income, so it may not be possible for everyone given the median Australian income in 2022 was $65,000; nonetheless, the FIRE movement may be worth considering if you're looking to reach financial independence.

In his blog, Mr. Money Mustache suggests that the percentage of your income that you save and invest (referred to as your 'savings rate') can determine how many years you need to wait to retire (see table 2.6). This is a huge motivator for me, as I would love to have a passive income that covers my expenses. Furthermore, it provides time and freedom to do what I love, whether that be working on side projects or spending time with my family. Having money buys me time, which is way more valuable when you have little ones.

Practising living on a reduced income

Now that you've got your finances in order, consider practising living on a reduced income in preparation for parental leave.

Table 2.6: how your savings rate determines your
working years until retirement

Savings rate (%)	Working years until retirement
10	51
20	37
30	28
40	22
50	17
60	12.5
70	8.5
80	5.5
90	<3
100	0

SOURCE: MR MONEY MUSTACHE

If you're coupled, and you or your partner (or both) are planning on taking parental leave, now may be a great time to try to see what kind of lifestyle can be sustained with reduced cash flow you'll have in that period. This is often referred to as 'living on one income'.

If you're single or run your own business, this may be really hard to do. Attempting to live off of your projected parental leave payments may give you an idea of what cash flow would be like once you're on leave. Alternatively, putting aside money for ECEC payments can give you a buffer and an insight into what costs will be like in the future.

The better you can prepare ahead of time, the easier it will be once you have a baby.

Estate and life planning – wills, prenups and insurance, oh my!

Whenever you experience a big life event, it's worth taking the time to look at important documents and ensure they are up to date. No one ever knows when a catastrophic event may happen, such as a medical emergency, debilitating sickness or even death.

Now, this is not the sexiest conversation to have, but estate and life planning is crucial when you start a family. (Heck, it's important even prior to that! But now is as good a time as any.)

Regardless of if you are co-parenting or single, drafting these documents can help bring peace of mind, especially around unanticipated life events. None of these things are as fun as setting up a nursery or folding new baby clothes, but I can guarantee you won't have the energy to do this once bub comes, so if there's any way you can assess these things prior to the days of sleep deprivation, it's in your family's best interest. At the end of the day, the purpose of most of this documentation is to ensure that your wishes are followed and you can ensure a stress-free, financially secure future for your family.

Wills

I wrote my first will when I was leaving Canada to travel the world for a year. At the time I had my apartment, my motorcycle and some cash in my retirement and savings accounts. I had no dependants and both my parents were alive. My will gave me peace of mind knowing that if something happened to me, my loved ones wouldn't have to scramble to figure out who got what or how it should be divided. Instead, everything was documented.

However, fast-forward multiple years, a new partner, more savings, investments, a home and a new human to boot, I knew that my old will was not representative of what I wanted if I were to pass. So, I revised the document to ensure that both my partner and children (and anyone else I wanted to add to my will) would be looked after in the event of my death.

One major consideration is how you want your assets to be split. If your kids are younger, you may not want anything to be left to them but to the guardian who is caring for them in your absence (your partner or someone else). Alternatively, you may want to have money held in their name that they can access at a specific age.

Regardless of what your wishes are, knowing exactly what you want to leave behind is not just about organising your thoughts and others' inheritance – it's about making everyone else's lives easier while they are mourning you. There is nothing more stressful than having to navigate the legal stress of a loved one who has passed while you're processing grief.

Creating a will can provide peace of mind for your loved ones. You can draft up a will through a lawyer or solicitor, or use one of the many online platforms specialising in creating wills. Your local post office should also have a handy will kit you can fill out. There's really nothing stopping you from even handwriting a will, provided it's signed by you and witnessed by two other people (who cannot be beneficiaries and who also need to sign it); however, having it looked over by a professional is probably in your best interest, since it's an important document.

Prenuptial agreement

For those of you who may not have been with your partner for a long time but will be bound in the future as parents of a little human, it may be worth signing a prenup, especially if you are bringing assets into the relationship. A prenup is an agreement made by a couple regarding the ownership of their respective assets in the event that their relationship ends. Now, of course, this isn't something anyone wishes when entering a partnership, but you may want to consider how to protect yourself and your child before your lives and finances are intermingled.

Some couples do prenups prior to marriage or moving in together. Prenups can be quickly drafted by a professional (as a couple's prenuptial agreement must meet strict legal criteria for the document to be legally binding) to ensure that your and your partner's assets are protected in the event that you go your separate ways.

Insurance

It is good to revisit insurance when having a kid. Here is a good way to think about it: how do you want to insure your family in the case of loss of income, death or anything else that's unforeseen?

Some of the most common types of insurance are income, disability, life and health insurance. Each focuses on protecting your family in a different way. Income protection insurance can provide you with a monthly payment in the event that you can no longer work due to an injury or illness, whereas disability insurance usually provides you with a lump-sum payment. If you are terminally ill or pass, life insurance also pays a lump sum to your family or loved ones.

About 55% of Australians have health insurance (also known as private healthcare), which can minimise wait times on elective surgery and allow you to choose your surgeon. Some parents opt for the private healthcare system when having a baby (which we will talk about in chapter 3). There is often a 12-month waiting period to access private healthcare services related to pregnancy and birth, so looking into what you need ahead of time can be helpful.

When considering your health insurance coverage and costs, it may be wise to also calculate any changes to your income. You will be required to pay the Medicare levy (which funds the public healthcare system and is calculated at 2% of your taxable income) once your income exceeds an income threshold (see table 2.7 overleaf), and a Medicare levy surcharge during tax time (if you don't take out health insurance and your income exceeds another threshold, see table 2.8 overleaf). If you have private health insurance, you may be eligible for the private health insurance rebate, whereby the government contributes towards your premiums; this rebate is also dependent on your income.

Table 2.7: Medicare levy thresholds 2022-2023

Category	Lower threshold
Family taxable income	$40,939
Single-parent family taxable income	$24,276
Family taxable income with eligibility for senior and pensioners tax offset	$53,406

SOURCE: ATO

Table 2.8: Medicare levy surcharge income thresholds and rates 2024

Single income threshold	Family income threshold*	Medicare levy surcharge
$0-$93,000	$0-$186,000	0%
$93,001-$108,000	$186,001-$216,000	1%
$108,001-$144,000	$216,001-$288,000	1.25%
$144,001 and over	$288,001 and over	1.50%

*The zero rate threshold increases for singles and families by $1500 for every child after the first child. Families and individuals with taxable income below the lower threshold do not pay Medicare levy. The lower threshold increases by $3760 or $4700 (depending on what ATO webpage you look at) for each dependent child or student.

SOURCE: ATO

As you start to think about your birthing or adoption plan (or your partner's) and consider taking leave, it may be a good time to check if your private healthcare plan is representative of both your medical needs and your projected income in the future, noting that your income will change if you are taking an extended period of leave.

Advance directives

Advance directives specify desires you wish for your family to follow in the unlikely event that you enter into a medical situation in which you cannot communicate (such as a stroke). This document instructs your loved ones on what you may or may not want with regard to procedures and treatments. Having this all documented makes it easier for them to make informed decisions while also respecting your wishes.

Power of attorney

In anticipation of a medical emergency (such as being in a coma) in which you aren't able to make financial decisions, it is a good idea to draft up a power of attorney. This is a legal document appointing someone to make financial and legal decisions in your place if you aren't able to do so. This person, who could be a partner or trusted family member, would be able to act in your best interest to ensure that financial decisions can still be made as needed so your kid can continue their life and routine without having to stress.

Child protection plan

Of course, no one wants to think about their own death, but for the sake of our children it's probably best we do. A child protection plan is a legal document that appoints a guardian for your child in the case of your death (and your partner's if you have one). It also includes any medical information they would need to be aware of, any notes about how you wish your child to be raised and what opportunities you'd like them to have. It can even include a summary of your own financial values.

Some parents go as far as recording video capturing their thoughts, wishes and important life lessons dedicated to their child. It's actually a beautiful proactive way to ensure your child's wellbeing is looked after if you were to suddenly pass.

If you want to ensure someone particular doesn't receive guardianship (such as an abusive ex), it is crucial to get this documentation sorted.

Separation and divorce

So much time, effort and money can be spent in the process of separation and divorce. Regardless of the reasons for separation, if it's at all possible to amicably split any assets, this can reduce the stress and financial burden on you and your family. A good mindset to take into a separation or divorce is to consider what is in the kids' best interests and try to adjust your thinking accordingly. This way, even if there are differences of opinion, you are both considering how to help your children in the future, especially financially.

If the situation isn't amicable, there are a lot of resources available to navigate this challenging time, including the Services Australia and Family Relationships Online websites. But the very first step is to ensure you and your child are safe. You can call 1800RESPECT, a domestic family and sexual violence counselling service, or visit their website for support.

Applying for child support takes time to assess and process; therefore, applying early can ensure you get the support you need. There are two main types of child support. The first is the 'child support assessment', whereby how much child support will need to be paid and to whom is assessed for you. The second is 'self-managed child support', whereby you and the other person manage the payments yourselves. Seeking legal guidance or a financial counsellor during this time is advisable as there are many other aspects to consider, such as a division of assets, support and custody of your child. It's important to consider your and your child's financial security during this time.

Actionable steps

- Track your income, expenses and net worth and have an understanding of your overall finances.
- If partnered, discuss how you want to split your expenses and find a budgeting system that works for you.

- Ensure you have an emergency fund and work out how much you think you'll need for parental leave.
- Practise for parental leave and try to live on a reduced income if you anticipate a change in cashflow.
- Get your estate planning in order, including wills, insurance and child protection plan.

Jacqui
33 | one child (3) | Melbourne, Vic.

How did you prepare yourself financially for parenthood?

After a relationship breakdown in 2016, I lost over $200,000. This was due to making several bad financial choices when in that relationship. I didn't know about investing and depended wholly on my ex-partner to make the financial decisions.

This huge financial loss woke me up, and I decided to educate myself for both my sake and my future family. I was lucky my mum had left me with two properties in Kenya, which I kept instead of selling off. I then sought financial advice and read several books on financial literacy that have since empowered me financially.

What was the biggest financial challenge you needed to navigate?

I had just been made redundant but decided I was ready to have a family. I had saved money, which I used to finance it all. I decided not to make any rash decisions and sell any of my investments off. I thought I'd be unemployed for no more than three months; instead, I was without work for over a year. Luckily, my redundancy package and emergency fund helped finance my lifestyle at the time. I was scared, but being in a good financial position helped me confidently make the decision to start my family and not panic into making any rash decisions around selling any of my investments.

How did you navigate the costs of fertility?

I was fortunate enough not to have to go through IVF (in-vitro fertilisation). I found a known donor and used IUI (intra-uterine insemination), which is cheaper and not as invasive.

What is the biggest challenge of being a single parent?

Having no family in Australia. I've had to build a network of friends who are kind and supportive. I've been lucky meeting a partner in the last five months who's been a great addition to our family and understands what parenting entails.

What support is essential for your family?

My little one has speech and language delays, which required getting NDIS (National Disability Insurance Scheme) support for him. A lot of people said not to worry; however, as a parent, I know my child best. Get the support you think your child needs when they are younger as the NDIS process is long. This support has been crucial in supporting my child and his development.

Have you done any estate or life planning?

Yes. Before he was born, I rewrote my will. I currently have life insurance and permanent and temporary disability insurance. Finally, as a single parent, I've found two loved ones I trust wholly to become guardians if anything happened to me.

How are you thinking about generational wealth for your child?

I am looking to teach my child about saving, spending and sharing when he is old enough to grasp the idea of money. I am looking to build a nest egg for us that will help him when his older, but more importantly teach him how to manage his own money. I currently invest in shares and property and am looking to buy our family home in the next three years, and build property in Kenya to rent out on land left to me by my grandma.

What do you wish you knew prior to becoming a parent?

I went into having a child scared yet certain this was what I wanted. I created an annual budget and bought essential items prior to his arrival, but I still wasn't prepared enough. You never will be, and that's okay. I think that's what I came out of this knowing. Each day brings its own financial and emotional challenges, and the best we can do is be present through them all.

Do you have any advice for new parents?

Parenthood is a joy but also difficult, and sometimes we are met with unexpected challenges. I've experienced pregnancy loss, and now I have a three-year-old who is a sweet, funny, goofy toddler who makes me go from laughing to wanting to pull my hair out in a matter of seconds. He has challenges that make me worry about him, but then he smiles and calls me 'Chaqui' instead of 'Mama' and I think how lucky I am to call him my child as we journey through this life together.

Jodie

29 | partner James (28), expecting | Hamilton, Vic.

Is your approach to finances similar to your partner's when it comes to planning for your family?

The biggest barrier between us is that my partner is a smoker and I am not. We both agree with how we would like to do things financially, but often it comes down to my income paying for things as my partner doesn't have as much leftover income.

We are in a strange financial position: I am on a full-time salary, however my partner works for his family and most of the time doesn't take home money but gets other benefits (such as a business card that pays for our groceries or his fuel and car expenses).

How did you start to think about finances before starting a family?

We both knew early on we wanted kids. We chose to buy a house (pre-COVID-19) over renting due to rent being the same or more than what our mortgage would be. We chose to buy well within our means (only 8 months into the relationship at this point); then it wasn't as big of a financial issue if anything happened between us, because either of us could have paid the mortgage on our own. We waited until everything was fully approved and the contract signed before I went off the pill to start trying for kids, knowing that a child would impact borrowing capacity.

After that, we didn't really think much about finances related to a child until 12 months of trying with no success and we had to start investigating why nothing was happening.

How has the cost of IVF impacted your finances?

Towards the end of the first year of trying, I started using ovulation trackers, which I think was about $30 a month. After 12 months of nothing happening I went to a gynaecologist (approximately $200 every visit, and over the course of two years I think I had five visits). They sent me to have my tubes flushed (approximately $150 after Medicare). I did six rounds of ovulation induction ($200 per cycle plus $50 trigger injection each round), and IVF cost us about $11,000 up front (with about $5500 back with Medicare). Adding a $1000 hospital fee, $1000 anaesthetic fee, $150 for medication, $800 for ICSI (injecting sperm directly into the egg) and $500 for egg freezing, it was about $11,500 all up.

Once I was confirmed pregnant, I had very low progesterone, which resulted in more medication – approximately $150 per week for five weeks. I also had a laparoscopy, which was fully covered by the public health system (after about a three-month wait).

The biggest impact for us was not knowing how long it would go on for and how many cycles we would have to do. We were very lucky that our first transfer stuck and we also had six embryos fit for freezing.

My boss has also been through IVF and so was very understanding with any time off work needed at short notice, and immediately put me on light duties once pregnant. (I work on a dairy farm, so it's usually a pretty physical job.)

We refinanced our house to help fund the IVF not knowing how much IVF was going to cost in the long run. Due to buying pre-COVID-19, our house had gone up $130,000 in value. We also have some cattle and we sold two of our cows for quick cash at the start of the IVF process.

What are your plans for parental leave?

I will take the government maternity leave, and once that finishes I will go back to work part-time, probably two days a week. My partner works mostly for his family and does a bit of shearing elsewhere, and so is very flexible with his work and can work around whenever I choose to work. We don't plan on using child care but will take our child to play group or something of the sort to have social time with other little kids. We have very low essential bills and can therefore get by on quite low incomes.

How are you thinking about generational wealth for your child?

I have just started dipping my toes into micro investing on my own as it's not something that really interests my partner. I also plan on adding extra into my super from a hair and beauty side hustle that I do.

My partner, along with his brother, will inherit their family farms, which will then get passed onto any kids in our families if they're interested. As for teaching about money, we both believe in good work ethic and working for your money, so we don't want to just hand money to our kids, but they will have the opportunity to help on the farm or do chores around the house for money. Also, we will be open about money and budgeting to help our kids understand the value of it.

Is there anything you wish you knew prior to having kids?

For us it was mostly the costs around IVF and infertility that we had no idea about. It was very hard to get an idea of what it would cost because it varies so much depending on how many rounds people have to do, where they go and any complications they may have. Having had a lot of family and friends with kids already, the general costs of kids aren't too much of a surprise – although the baby isn't here yet, so we could have plenty of surprises later!

Do you have any advice for anyone contemplating parenthood?

Don't be afraid to seek help or speak up if something isn't working. Around us, no one speaks of IVF or infertility until you mention it, and then you would be surprised how many people have experienced it. It is something that definitely needs to be spoken about a lot more, as well as any complications during the pregnancy or birth.

Chapter 3

The cost of having kids

'Wealth is the ability to fully experience life.'
Henry David Thoreau

The first year of parenthood is a rollercoaster of emotions. Some people are pumped full of oxytocin, while others fall into depression. Now pair those highs and lows with sleep deprivation and things can get a bit hectic. So, it's important in that first year to reduce as much financial stress as possible to focus on what's most important: you and your baby.

Let's talk about the cost of having kids. There's not much recent data on the cost of raising children in Australia, and the research that is out there was either collated prior to COVID-19 or has a small sample size. Nonetheless, let's dive into the numbers.

A 2018 study by the Australian Institute of Family Studies estimates that for unemployed or low-income families the weekly cost of raising two children is between $280 and $340. That amount ranges from $262,080 to $318,240 for two children for 18 years. However, a 2013 report by the University of Canberra profiled three different families and income brackets and found that the cost of raising two children for a typical middle-income family is $812,000. The research found that costs ranged from $474,000 for low-income families to $1,097,000 for high-income families, which is a huge spread. In a 2021 study, Suncorp stated that in the last five years, the cost of raising a child has increased more than 10%, which would then increase the cost of raising an average two-child family to $893,200 in 2021. And surely the cost of living and raising a child has gone up since then. Yeesh.

I think we can all agree, kids ain't cheap. The sad reality is that children get more expensive as they grow. So, once you stop paying for early childhood education and care (ECEC), other expenses such as primary and secondary education, technology and extracurricular activities crop up. This is not to mention the need for more space, which makes rent and mortgage costs higher in comparison to our childless friends.

So, let's dive into some of the costs of raising a child.

Healthcare, birth and the cost of bringing a child into your life

Before you hold bub in your arms for the first time, chances are you've already started spending money on your little human. The cost of pregnancy and birth in Australia depends on a few factors, such as if you are planning on using the public or private system and what subsidies are available to you. If you're planning on using the private hospital system, it's best to reach out to your insurance provider to ensure that you are eligible, since most of them have a 12-month waiting period for obstetric services.

There isn't much data around the actual costs of giving birth in Australia due to the lack of data collection from patients accessing resources. This may make it harder for parents to plan accordingly. Luckily, most costs of pregnancy and birth are covered by Medicare with the exclusion of some scans, pathology tests and medicine. The estimated out-of-pocket cost of having a baby in the public system, which about 75% of pregnant women opt for, is up to $1500.

The private hospital out-of-pocket cost is much higher: between $2500 and $20,000 depending on the fees specialists set and what your health fund covers. Although Medicare does cover some costs, there is often a gap that parents need to pay, with the average being about $780. So, it's advantageous to speak with your provider to ensure you know the total out-of-pocket costs prior to accessing treatment.

For those who choose to have a home birth, the out-of-pocket cost is between $3500 and $6000, with midwives and doulas setting their own fees. Those who live in rural areas may need to contact their local GP and midwife and coordinate with local hospitals, the costs of which may vary.

None of these costs account for pregnancy preparations such as vitamins, birthing classes, pregnancy products and clothing, and any recovery treatment needed (including postnatal depression support or pelvic floor issues).

Pregnancy and birth aren't the only cost for many parents, especially in LGBTQIA+ families: almost one in 20 babies is born with the help of assisted reproductive technology. According to IVF Australia, one cycle of in-vitro fertilisation (IVF) costs $10,532, with out-of-pocket costs for an initial cycle estimated at $5483 and subsequent cycles being only slightly cheaper at $4898 per treatment. Of course, it's possible that multiple IVF treatments are needed or other procedures as well, such as frozen embryo transfer and intracytoplasmic sperm injection, each coming with its own cost. For so many families, the costs can really add up before bub is even born.

For those considering surrogacy, altruistic surrogacy is legal in Australian states and territories, which means that surrogates are not paid to carry a baby, but the intending parents usually cover the costs related to pregnancy and surrogacy.

As for the cost of adoption, fees are between $3000 and $10,000 per application, plus there may be additional costs such as preparation of documents, travel and translation, especially if the adoption is taking place overseas.

The good news is that with a bit of planning ahead and an understanding of the range of options available, you can keep costs to a minimum and ensure you budget for anything unexpected.

Budgeting for baby

Research by Choice, a consumer advocacy group, estimates that 'for the first four years of your baby's life, you could spend more than $3500 a year on baby purchases, or almost $8000 a year including childcare', whereas Canstar estimates that the first year of parenthood can cost you between $4310 and $9620. For those with twins, in the first year, the cost is around $13,000 more than a single birth (not accounting for medical costs or complications). This includes anything that's directly related to a baby – including furniture, clothes and nappies. What it doesn't include is all the indirect costs, such as housing, transportation and utilities, which are often higher than before baby as more space, travel and temperature regulation is needed with the addition of a new human (see table 3.1). Then, of course, there's the time taken off from work, which affects the household income.

Table 3.1: estimates of expenses in baby's first year

Expense in baby's first year	Lower estimate	Upper estimate
Setting up your home	$500	$2600
Nappies	$1000	$2800
Food for baby	$1060	$2470
Maternity wear	$250	$250
Baby wear	$500	$500
Transport	$1000	$1000
Total	$4310	$9620

SOURCE: CANSTAR

More than half of parents in another study reported that starting a family is more expensive than they previously expected and, with the costs of consumer goods and ECEC rising, the outlay can be astronomical. In my case, I was prepared for the cost of ECEC but was still blown away when I saw the equivalent of my rent payments being taken out of my account every week for my kid. But I'll talk more about the cost of ECEC in chapter 5. The truth is that every little cost adds up. Surely no one even thinks to budget for the cost of a birth certificate and passport, but even identification costs money.

Let's break down some of the costs.

Baby necessities, environmental impact and keeping costs low

In 2023, the Australian baby and child market amounted to $14.21 billion. This industry is a massive marketing machine, playing on your feelings and desires and marking up the price, knowing parents make emotional financial decisions in the months leading up to birth.

It's not uncommon to hear parents say that their child deserves the best. I've even had friends tell me that they only want their child wearing a specific organic cotton clothing brand. And I get it – our little humans are indeed precious and we want the best for them. But that doesn't mean we need to sacrifice our wallets in the process.

The reality is that all your bub needs is a safe place to sleep, a safe way to travel, food, clothes, and, of course, your love and attention. In fact, the chances are that most of the physical items your baby needs already exist and have only been used for a handful of weeks (or, at most, months). It's true that not having children has a greater environmental impact than being car free or even reducing international travel; so if you are having kids and it's possible to be more environmentally conscientious while also saving money, why wouldn't you?

One of the best ways to consider both the planet and your wallet is by seeking second-hand items. Of course, safety and hygiene are important, so you might choose to buy a new mattress and car seat (or buy them second-hand from a reliable source), but many other items can easily be sourced second-hand.

Besides visiting the local op shop, there are many online Buy Nothing and mum groups where people give away second-hand items or sell them very cheaply in order to declutter their space. (That's the way I got most of my kids' clothes and, frankly, I was also more than eager to pass on clothes to my friends once we were done with them.) The baby community is one of the friendliest and most supportive I've come across. I've even had a mum drop off some bottles for me as it was on her way and, in her words, she 'understands the exhaustion new mothers experience'. How gorgeous, right?

So, what are some of the necessities that you may need to budget for (or can score second-hand)? I've put together a list (see table 3.2).

Table 3.2: baby necessities

Item	Condition	Comment
Maternity clothes	Used	These are worn for no more than a few months.
Bassinet and cot	Used	To save money, you can opt to just use a cot and pass on a bassinet (seeing as it's only used for a few months).
Mattress	New	Recommended new or from a trusted source for hygiene reasons.
Car seat	New	Recommended new or from a trusted source such as family or a reliable second-hand provider for safety purposes.
Pram	Used	There are a lot of second-hand options.

Item	Condition	Comment
Nappies and baby wipes	New	Reusables are both economical and environmental.
Baby clothes	Used	In the first year bub grows so quickly that sometimes they don't even get to wear everything before they grow out of the size. You can often find brand-new baby clothes even at second-hand stores.
Change table	Used	Consider using the top of a chest of drawers with an inexpensive change cushion.
High chair	Used	Again, there are lots of great second-hand options.
After-birth sanitary pads or period undies	New	There are great reusable options you can use once your period returns too.
Nipple pads	New	Reusable options are available.
Breast pump and bottles, and cleaning supplies (if planning to pump)	New/used	Lots of second-hand options are available.
Toys	Used	Bub will not play with toys for quite a while, so most important for the first 6 months is a play mat (for tummy time). There are also lots of options from online marketplaces, parents' groups and toy libraries.

The trick I found for getting the items I really wanted on Facebook Marketplace, eBay or Gumtree was to set an alert for a specific item I was looking for. Many high-end children's brands have good resale value, so you can buy second-hand, use the item and then sell it for the same price you originally bought it for.

Remember that companies want you to buy more. They pull at your heartstrings, stating that your baby deserves the very best – that you need to purchase that special organic cotton onesie handsewn using only the most sustainable soft bamboo fabric crafted by vegan angels on an eco-cloud in heaven – and you shouldn't settle for anything less. Don't fall for their marketing. In fact, some of the best advice I received from a friend when purchasing items prior to having baby was, 'Don't buy it unless you're sure you absolutely need it'. This saved me so much time and money, as I often found that I really didn't need that item I was deliberating over at Baby Bunting. On the environmental impact side, second-hand is greenest. Anything new, organic or not, just results in more stuff eventually ending up in landfill.

Food, formula and breastmilk

Feeding small humans is expensive, and as they get older the cost of food increases as well. On average parents spend $402 a month feeding their child, and that will most likely continue to increase with inflation. There are a lot of budget-friendly options to reduce food costs, such as bulk-cooking and choosing plant-based options, which are both environmentally friendlier and cheaper than eating animal products. But before kids are eating a varied diet, chances are they start on formula or breastmilk.

For parents who opt for formula, the cost can be between $1500 and $2000 a year to feed a baby. This includes formula, bottles and cleaning supplies. Although it's more expensive than breastmilk, it can help free up time and allow multiple people to feed the baby.

Breastmilk advocates often state that breastmilk is free, but although it is a cheaper option, it doesn't come without disadvantages. Breastfeeding can come with its own challenges in terms of discomfort and production. On top of that, it is time-consuming: one year of breastfeeding equates to about 1800 hours of a mother's time. That's almost a full-time job if you consider a 40-hour work week with three weeks of vacation, which is about 1960 hours of work a year. So, next time someone states that breastfeeding is free, remind them that it's only free if you don't value a mother's time. (Time is money, isn't it?) And of course, breastfeeding isn't necessarily free; for those who can't nurse, there's the cost of pumps, bottles and breastfeeding consultants. Everything comes with a cost.

There are pros and cons for each option of what to feed children, but ultimately, fed is best, regardless of which option you choose.

Nappies

For any new parent, it's obvious that nappies take up a huge part of the baby budget. In total, disposable nappies can cost around $3771 until undies are introduced. Reusable nappies have a larger upfront cost of about $1000, but decrease in cost per use, especially if reused with additional children. Reusable nappies are more environmentally friendly even when the washing costs are taken into consideration, especially since their counterpart uses plastic components that take an estimated 150 to 500 years to fully decompose, with 1.5 billion discarded in landfills each year in Australia. Nappies, regardless of type, is a cost to add to the budget in the early years, but luckily you can reduce it if you are able to potty train your child early.

Celebrating baby – babymoon and baby shower

If you're in the planning stage of having a baby or adopting, you may consider a babymoon or baby shower.

A babymoon is a great opportunity to connect with your partner and enjoy the last moments of being childless. These trips can be expensive for couples who opt to travel overseas; a local trip is likely to be easier on the budget while still providing an opportunity to share a special time together and get some sleep-ins before the baby arrives.

A baby shower is a great way to celebrate with family and friends. It can vary in cost, with the average cost hovering around $591. However, these events can be as cheap or as expensive as you allow them to be. Also, guests love to shower expecting parents with gifts, which saves you money as well.

The indirect costs – housing, utilities and transportation

Most research focuses on the direct costs of having a child (such as nappies and clothes), which are easy to account for. However, there is a whole bunch of indirect costs that can add up when having a family. In fact, parents are most financially stressed about mortgage and rent payments, groceries, and utilities and rates, in that order (see figure 3.1).

Figure 3.1: financial stressors for Australian families

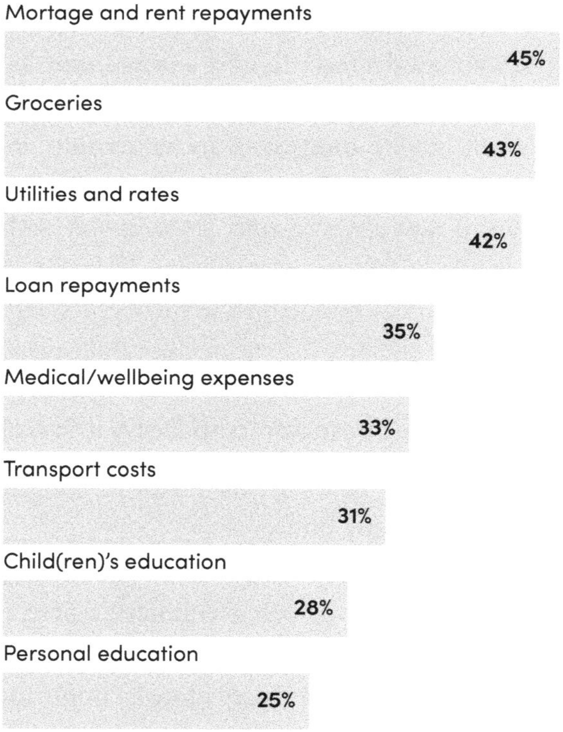

Mortage and rent repayments

45%

Groceries

43%

Utilities and rates

42%

Loan repayments

35%

Medical/wellbeing expenses

33%

Transport costs

31%

Child(ren)'s education

28%

Personal education

25%

SOURCE: FUTURITY INVESTMENT GROUP

Luckily, there are things you can do to reduce some of these expenses.

Housing

As new members are added to a household, more space is often needed, and housing costs increase as a result. Adding a new room, more storage space and a backyard can increase housing expenses by hundreds if not thousands of dollars, not to mention moving costs and possibly more furniture to fit out the space. Finding a suitable rental can be stressful at the best of times; doing so with a young family can feel like a struggle and be more expensive, especially if you have a child with special needs. Although not everyone can afford an upgrade in living space, rent and mortgages are still the single biggest line item in a family's budget.

One of the things to consider when moving and upgrading is being conscious of the area you move to and its proximity to work and schools. Some families choose to move further from the city, as they can afford a larger property, but this can come with other costs, such as the need for more vehicles and fuel to get to work and school. An important factor to keep in mind is that if you move to where you need to buy a car (or second car), that additional cost can be more than what you save in rent or mortgage repayments.

Also, when considering moving to a new suburb, it's worth doing a cost-benefit analysis on the price of property compared with the schools in the area. Some suburbs are more expensive but have great public schools which means you may be paying more for property but could potentially save on education costs. Alternatively, living in a cheaper suburb to reduce housing costs may allow you to pay high independent (private) school fees. It's always good to weigh up the options and see what works best for you and your family based on your priorities.

Depending on if you commute to work, the proximity of your house to your workplace or public transport may be important. However, as more companies become open to remote working options, you may find that your proximity to schools is more important. I know that when my family moved, at first I was obsessed with being close to transit, but I then realised that what I really needed was to be close to ECEC and schools, as I was able to work remotely from home but my kids will go to school five days a week without fail.

Also, regardless of if you have a mortgage or pay rent, it is always worth asking to reduce your rate. For mortgages, just call up your bank or broker and see if they can offer you a better rate. Sometimes it's worth shopping around as well. Often banks provide better rates to new customers and expect old customers to stay loyal and pay a higher amount. (This is referred to as the loyalty tax.) If you're renting, signing a contract for a longer time period can lock in a price and avoid the price hikes that landlords tend to dish out regularly.

Gas and electricity

Gas and electricity continue to rise in price and, although at the time of writing it's forecast that electricity prices will reduce, future costs are uncertain. However, electric-powered appliances and cars are among the best options for both your wallet and the climate as they cost less than half as much to run as fossil-fuel options.

With additional family members, energy consumption increases. Just think, it's recommended to keep a baby's room at 18 to 22 degrees Celsius for a safe sleeping environment, so in Australia this often means that either heating or air conditioning needs to be used, which increases the overall household expenses. For adults, it may be easy to throw on a jumper or throw off the covers, but for little humans we need to constantly consider their needs, which unfortunately often comes with high costs. It's also worth shopping around for better deals when it comes to energy. The Australian Energy Regulator's comparison tool at Energy Made Easy and the Victorian Energy Compare website are great ways to compare companies and costs.

There are some options to reduce your energy consumption and costs. The initial installation costs for some of these may be quite expensive, but over a long period of time they will reduce your costs and your impact on the climate, and even improve your family's health. Table 3.3 and figure 3.2 show some options worth considering.

Table 3.3: energy cost-reduction options

Item	Comment	Housing type
LED lights	Replacing existing lights with LED lights reduces costs because they use less energy.*	Rental/owner-occupied
Insulation	Insulation can help regulate the temperature in your home. Even rugs and curtains help!	Rental/owner-occupied
Draught sealing	This reduces the amount of hot and cold air escaping by closing gaps in windows and doors.	Rental/ owner-occupied
Using appliances during off-peak hours	This reduces the cost of appliance use during energy surge pricing.	Rental/owner-occupied
Heat-pump dryer	Swapping a vented dryer for a heat-pump dryer (or better yet, air-dry!) can reduce long-term costs.*	Rental/owner-occupied
Split-system heating and cooling	This uses heat-pump technology, which uses less energy than gas heating.*	Owner-occupied
Induction cooktop	Replace gas cooktops, which cause up to 12% of asthma cases in children, with induction cooktops.	Owner-occupied
Heat-pump or solar for hot water	Again, this can reduce overall costs and is more environmentally friendly.	Owner-occupied
Solar panels	Installing solar panels on your rooftop reduces energy costs.	Owner-occupied

*Some of these are supported by government subsidy programs. Check if a program is available in your state or territory.

Figure 3.2: Australian home running costs – conventional versus electrified

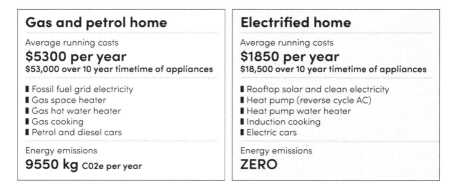

Gas and petrol home

Average running costs
$5300 per year
$53,000 over 10 year timetime of appliances

▮ Fossil fuel grid electricity
▮ Gas space heater
▮ Gas hot water heater
▮ Gas cooking
▮ Petrol and diesel cars

Energy emissions
9550 kg CO_2e per year

Electrified home

Average running costs
$1850 per year
$18,500 over 10 year timetime of appliances

▮ Rooftop solar and clean electricity
▮ Heat pump (reverse cycle AC)
▮ Heat pump water heater
▮ Induction cooking
▮ Electric cars

Energy emissions
ZERO

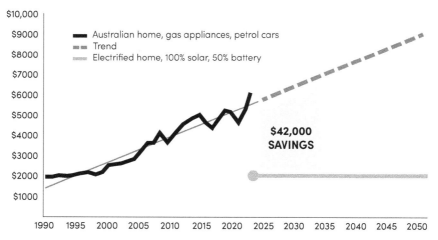

SOURCE: REWIRING AUSTRALIA

Although some of these options aren't available to renters, they may be worth considering in the future if your living situation changes. In the meantime, it's also worth shopping around for the best prices on utilities to take advantage of offers for new customers.

Cars and transportation

Even if you work from home, chances are you'll have to chauffeur your child to and from ECEC or school regularly. This adds to petrol costs, insurance and overall wear and tear of a car (because nothing makes a car lose its newness like crumbs and sticky hands). A 2021 Finder survey found that parents spend on average 3.5 hours a week driving their children to school and other activities. Not only does this mean the cost of transportation goes up but your available time as a parent decreases. Why did we decide to be parents, again? (Joke, joke… but not really.)

Many parents also opt for a second car to provide flexibility and need to consider a reliable car that is spacious enough to fit a car seat (or three!). Adding an additional vehicle increases costs significantly, including petrol, maintenance and insurance expenses. To keep costs low, use petrol apps that compare prices of fuel and remember to look for cheaper insurance deals annually.

Some states and territories are incentivising the move to electric cars with subsidies to reduce the environmental impact, which could be a consideration for some families. Electric bikes are also becoming a popular way for parents to do ECEC and school runs, grab groceries and run errands.

Travelling with little humans

As someone who loves to travel, my budget for adventuring with kids is shockingly expensive now in comparison to when I was childfree. Not only is it logistically challenging (how do you strap a baby to your body while carrying luggage and negotiating with a toddler to not run off?), it's so much effort. Really, it's not a holiday – it's basically caring for your kids in an unfamiliar environment. That being said, 94% of families view holidays as an opportunity for children to experience the world.

Flying with a bub under two is cheaper as airlines often provide them with free travel if they are seated on your lap. For international flights, be aware that there is usually a fee included. Parents estimate spending $2563 per year for holidays with children and often need to consider kid-friendly travel destinations, accommodation and length of stay as well.

Although travelling with kids is absolutely rewarding in terms of creating long-lasting memories together, more than half of parents miss having the types of vacations they used to prior to becoming parents. I know I do.

Unpaid leave due to sick days and school holidays

It's often easy to forget to calculate the loss in income from taking unpaid leave as it's not a direct expense in the way purchasing a car seat or paying for ECEC is. However, this can be considered a true opportunity cost as it's the potential forgone profit of employment. We will talk more about parental leave and what to expect in chapter 4.

Balancing sick days and care

Once parental leave comes to an end, the likelihood that you will have to take sick days is very high. With the introduction of ECEC or school, kids often are exposed to new viruses that make them sick, and in turn you may need to take carer's leave days in order to look after them.

A 2017 study showed that in 90% of cases mothers are expected to stay home to look after sick children, while fathers do so only 10% of the time. Often these working mothers are using annual leave instead of their partner using sick or carer's leave. In some cases, sick kids are sent to school because there are no more carer's leave days to access.

So, what are your rights?

In Australia, full-time employees are entitled to ten days of paid sick and carer's leave, and that's pro-rata for part-time employees. Sick and carer's leave – also referred to as personal leave – allows you to take time off for personal illness, caring responsibilities or family emergencies. You are also entitled to two days of unpaid carer's leave, whether you're a casual or full-time worker. Any unused sick days are carried over to the next year.

Although it's never easy to juggle work and caring for a sick child, there may be some ways to mitigate the stress by splitting the duties equally with your partner (if you have one) or reaching out to friends and family who may step in to help when you can't miss a deadline and need to work. Also, if it's available to you, you may request adjusted hours or attempt to juggle working from home with caring duties in extenuating circumstances. Another option, though much more expensive, is opting for hired help such as a babysitter or nanny who can step in to help when the kids are sick but you need to work.

Annual leave and unpaid leave

School children have a lot of breaks between their school terms. This often results in parents taking annual leave in order to sync up their holidays with breaks. Some parents may need to coordinate leave days in order to ensure someone is available when the kids are home (especially when they are young). Also, these breaks are when most families go on holiday, resulting in high travel costs. Long gone are the childless days of taking holidays whenever it suits you; now some strategic planning and coordinating is required.

Unpaid domestic duties

It's worth noting that with kids comes a lot of extra housework: laundry, food prep and, of course, the endless cleaning. Also, childcaring takes so much effort in the first few years, supporting little ones with nappies, bathing, dressing and everything their chubby little hands can't seem to coordinate themselves. It's unfortunate that women predominantly take on this role, spending twice as much time on domestic duties as men, even when working the same hours. Same-gender couples divide the domestic and parenting duties more equitably in comparison, as do trans and non-binary parents. The truth is, our society isn't built to support families on a single income; therefore, domestic duties and care often fall disproportionately on one person, even if they are working. Achieving an egalitarian division of labour may be a challenge, but it is something to be cognisant of.

The cost of education

Many parents are shocked at the cost of ECEC fees. A report by the Australian Competition and Consumer Commission (ACCC) found that for 50% of households that are low-income, the cost of ECEC is between 5% and 21%, or more, of their disposable income. Compare this to high-income households, where it's between 2% and 9%. In the same 2023 study, it was confirmed that ECEC fees outpaced both inflation and wage growth over the last four years. Although new parents often think that budgeting gets easier once kids are out of ECEC as it makes room for more cash flow, the truth is that kids do get more expensive as they get older when factoring all costs including food, extracurricular activities and, of course, education. Almost half of all parents feel that they didn't save enough for their child's education, and those who rank themselves as having lower financial literacy feel the most financial strain, making it apparent that planning ahead can be beneficial.

About 86% of parents believe that education is important for their child to thrive, so it's no surprise that parents need to weigh up cost versus value when it comes to schools. For many parents, the quality of teachers is the top priority when choosing the right school for their child. As not all schools are alike, it's always advantageous to take a tour to see what is best for your child's needs; just because a school is privately funded doesn't mean it's the best in the area, and the same is true of government schools. With changes to principals, teachers and staff, schools can shift in culture and quality, so being open-minded may help you to find something that suits your child's needs. Nonetheless, education does come with a cost regardless of which option you choose, hence why 50% of parents are very intentional about planning financially for their child's education.

The cost of education varies due to the type of school your child attends, which state or territory you live in and if you are based in a city or regionally. Regional schools are more affordable than major cities, and independent (private) schools are the most expensive, followed by Catholic and then public (see table 3.4).

In 2023, the average cost of a 13-year public education is $84,554, whereas it's $173,706 for Catholic schools and a whopping $288,880 if you send your child to an independent school (see figure 3.3). The cost of education can have a negative impact on many families, especially those who opt for more expensive options, and statistically the families that suffer the most are those who have lower financial literacy. In fact, only 18% of parents stated that education costs had no negative impact on them. (I'm assuming those are the rich folks, bless their hearts.)

Table 3.4: national annual average of tuition fees
by school type and stage in 2023

	Government schools	Catholic schools	Independent schools
Primary	$221	$2132	$6541
Secondary	$536	$5477	$11,553

SOURCE: FUTURITY

Figure 3.3: average total cost of a 13-year education

Government schools
$84,554
Catholic schools
$173,706
Independent schools
$288,880

SOURCE: FUTURITY

For single parents, education costs can impact their bottom line substantially, with 60% of single parents choosing not to purchase items for themselves and 40% struggling to pay bills with rising costs.

But there are other costs besides the cost of tuition, including the cost of uniforms, school excursions, books, sporting equipment and transportation. All of those add up to an annual average cost per child of $2325 for primary school and $4212 for secondary school (see figure 3.4). That totals a national spend of $11.4 billion.

Figure 3.4: average annual school costs per student 2023

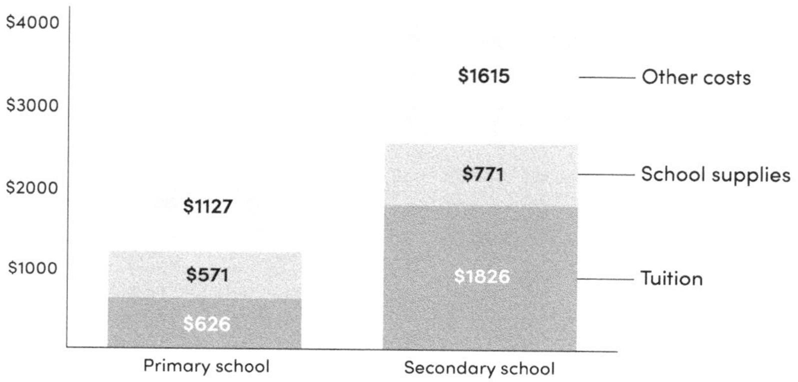

It's not surprising that 47% of parents were not aware of all of the costs associated with enrolling a child into school. I know I had no clue until doing this research (but maybe that's because I didn't go to school in Australia).

Public schools

Public schooling is unfortunately not free, as many believe, because the additional costs as mentioned above (uniforms, excursions and books) need to be accounted for when considering the overall cost of education. Depending on where you live, tuition can differ by tens of thousands of dollars between government schools, with Melbourne being the most expensive city in Australia at $102,807 over the course of a child's 13 years of education. Research conducted by Finder in 2023 found that out of the 1000-plus parents they surveyed, 10% of parents had switched their kids to public education from private and 17% were contemplating it.

Catholic schools

About 20% of Australian students are educated through the Catholic school system, with Canberra being the most expensive city for a child to obtain a Catholic education at around $197,667 – 7% above the national average. Catholic schools are often seen as a mid-cost option for those who want to send their kids to an independent school but can't afford the cost.

Independent (private) schools

It's no surprise that Sydney is the most expensive city for independent education, with the huge price tag of $357,931 per child over the course of their schooling being 19% above the national average (see table 3.5). Tuition is the highest cost, but then there's still tutoring, equipment, books and uniforms to account for (see table 3.6 overleaf).

Table 3.5: total estimated cost of education for a child starting school in 2023

Location	Government	Catholic	Independent
National (metro)	$87,528	$184,545	$300,233
National (regional and remote)	$75,795	$163,578	$209,584
Canberra	$77,002	$197,667	$275,486
Sydney	$89,500	$178,478	$357,931
NSW (regional and remote)	$82,823	$158,553	$218,732
Brisbane	$80,419	$193,235	$262,531

... continued

Location	Government	Catholic	Independent
Qld (regional and remote)	$68,597	$154,661	$196,876
Adelaide	$83,306	$186,350	$273,435
SA (regional and remote)	$81,824	$157,025	$238,625
Melbourne	$102,807	$184,366	$307,508
Vic. (regional and remote)	$75,217	$165,262	$208,057
Perth	$85,701	$191,397	$213,889
WA (regional and remote)	$70,774	$165,889	$198,507

SOURCE: FUTURITY

Table 3.6: top five most common ancillary costs

Stage	School uniform	Stationery	School excursions	Sports uniform	Electronic devices
Government primary school	$212	$118	$132	$142	$725
Government secondary school	$264	$113	$151	$181	$828
Catholic primary school	$323	$135	$242	$231	$884
Catholic secondary school	$494	$128	$279	$215	$1172
Independent primary school	$315	$159	$174	$306	$1042
Independent secondary school	$1046	$496	$786	$489	$1201

SOURCE: FUTURITY

Extracurricular activities, gifts and technology

A 2020 study found that parents pay $1859 a year on average for their kids' extracurricular activities. That's $3.8 billion nationwide that parents fork out. Although activities can vary in cost, from as low as $270 a year (Scouts) to as much as $3280 (equestrian), they often get more expensive as your kids grow and become more serious about their craft. Not to mention uniforms, shoes and travel to games and performances all add to costs. But for a lot of parents, having their kids involved in these activities is a benefit as it fosters community, helps to develop confidence and ultimately keeps their kids off screens. Some parents also opt for investing in a tutor to help their child navigate their educational obligations.

Birthday parties and gifts add to the growing costs of children. On average parents spend $320 on their child's birthday party and $232 on gifts. As for their children's friends, they spend an average of $46 on gifts and they attend about 8 parties per year, which can total to $368 in gifts for your kid's friends. Now, let's not forget about Christmas, when on average parents spend $222 per child, and Easter, when they spend $38 per child. That's over $1100 in parties and gifts for just one child for one year.

But the truth is that it's just so easy to spoil kids, and research shows that parents in fact want to spoil their kids. I know that I'm definitely more willing to purchase my kids a new book or toy than buy something for myself because I love seeing them get excited. It's so hard to curb that desire.

Another budget item that has grown over the last five years is technology. Parents spend about $106 per child per month on tech and communication devices and plans, including mobile phones, computers and gaming consoles. In some cases, schools expect students to have access to various devices for educational needs, and over the course of their child's education parents are expected to pay over $7000 for devices.

On top of all these costs, there's also the expectation that parents provide an allowance or spending money, which can add up over the years. I cover some of this in Chapter 8.

Medical and special needs considerations

Children are expensive as it is, but with additional needs, more costs can accrue. Everything from glasses to orthodontist appointments, from neurodivergent support to counselling sessions, unfortunately are not covered fully by Medicare, meaning more out-of-pocket costs that impact a family and their budget. It's no surprise, then, that parents of children with special needs often find that parenting is significantly more expensive than they initially anticipated and are more likely to say that they struggle financially. The best you can do is to have as much buffer as possible for unexpected costs for your child. Their health and happiness is of utmost importance, and as parents it can be hard to balance budgets to ensure that our kids get the support they need.

Actionable steps

- Create an estimated budget for the first year of baby's arrival.
- Review your expenses and attempt to reduce them. Challenge yourself to negotiate a lower mortgage rate, shop around for better energy prices or save some money on groceries.
- Estimate how much you think your child will cost you per year (including education costs) to help anticipate future expenses.

Mastura

35 | husband (38), three kids (13, 11 and 7) | Perth, WA

How did you prepare yourself financially for parenthood?

I was 21 when I had my first child, right before I turned 22. Finance was not something that was given much thought and I did not know what I know now.

How did you and your partner approach planning financially for your family's future?

From the beginning of our relationship, I was always the one who managed the finances. I drove a lot of our financial decision-making, but at the same time, we talked through a lot of it together. For the first few years we were married, we kept separate accounts, but I grew tired of transferring back and forth between accounts, so in the end we opened a joint bank account and closed off our separate accounts. We had a rough budget and always paid our bills before anything else, but it wasn't overly strict.

There was a point when my husband asked why we didn't have much left over to spend, and I explained to him the way I did budgeting and how I allocated funds. I also asked him to take it over for a while so he understood not only what I did and why but also had the opportunity to find efficiencies or different ways he was comfortable budgeting for our family. After this exercise, he understood the task of managing the finances and was happy to give it back to me to manage going forward. It made us focus together on what we wanted to work towards as a family and how we would achieve them.

Do you and your partner have a similar money mindset?

I believe so. For both of us, our parents didn't talk to us much about money, but we did grow up with the usual remark of 'money doesn't grow on trees'. For both of us, both parents worked when we were younger, and we didn't feel as though we were without.

How did you navigate parental leave?

I went back to work when my daughter was seven months old because the payments I received (such as the Baby Bonus) allowed me to stay home for that long. With my second child, I went back when he was five months old, and with my youngest I went back when he was just three months old. That was so difficult and one of the hardest things I had to do, but it was necessary as we needed that additional source of income.

We were lucky that my mother in law was able to look after the kids. My daughter did go to childcare two days a week and we had some of this rebated, but the cost was still high and we needed to consider the amount we needed to pay to keep her there.

What advice would you give to new parents?

Consider saving a bit for maternity and parental leave. I wish I saved more money before we had children; it would have been incredible to have saved enough to have both of us home, present and together in those first few months.

Also, I would suggest not buying too many things, as we bought some things that we didn't even use. Buy the main big items and decide what else you need along the way. My parents bought a cot and change table for us as a gift and either my parents or my in-laws bought us a bassinet. We bought the pram, car seat, high chair, breast pump and other baby items. Factor in the cost of nappies, formula and wipes for every shop. If you can breastfeed, try to keep doing that for as long as possible, as it is free milk.

What are your family's biggest financial challenges?

With a growing family, one of the biggest costs is your grocery bill. As your children grow, they consume much more than when they were littler. Other costs include the yearly school list, which can be a few hundred dollars every year, including books, school uniform and shoes. Throughout the year you have to pay for excursions, incursions and school activities. Also, eating out as a family and doing activities together can be quite costly.

What other costs do you need to consider?

Kids are receiving mobile phones really early – around nine or ten years old. My daughter was one of the last kids in her year to get a mobile phone and she was 11. And what you do for one child you need to do for the rest of them. Also, during COVID-19, when all the kids were at home, we bought them tablets to use for schoolwork. Although they don't cost anything to maintain, it was still a few hundred dollars to purchase each, and now they use them for their homework during the week.

We pay public transportation costs for my daughter as she takes the bus to and from high school. Another big cost is clothing, and because they are always growing you are always having to buy clothing that fits them. Our children also have extracurricular activities that we need to budget for, such as weekly swimming lessons (about $300 a month) and my boys play soccer ($400 to $500 a season, plus about $200 for new boots and gear each season).

We purchased our home with the First Home Owner's Grant and used a lender that allowed us to have a reduced deposit. We built our home, and we were lucky to be able to do that given we had two dependants already and another one on the way, which affected our borrowing capacity. We recently refinanced out of the high interest rate from this first home lender. However, we are considering housing again now given high schools only allow children to enrol if you live within the catchment (here in Perth, anyway) and most of the good schools are in the more affluent suburbs. We really want to move to an area that will allow our children access into these schools.

How do you budget for your ongoing costs?

We have a growing sinking fund (money set aside for emergencies, debts and other expenses) for all ongoing costs, which are factored into our monthly budget. In certain months of the year, I know the allocation for certain things will be higher, so I factor this into our budget. For example, towards the end of the year I am already planning for the next school year's costs.

Kaylie

32 | husband Dion (30), expecting |
Manly Beach, NSW

How did you think about finances before starting a family?

Our friends and family in the US had kids a lot younger, but we have never been in a rush. We enjoyed building our careers and have been able to travel quite extensively. Coming back to Sydney last year, we were both fortunate enough to find jobs at larger companies that have good family benefits, ranging from extended parental leave to fertility support and even parental coaching. This added security blanket gave us the nudge to give parenthood a go, which would have been more challenging if we were at smaller startups with fewer benefits. We were also realistic that waiting too long could have an impact on fertility, which is costly financially and even more so emotionally. We have tracked our income and expenses on a monthly basis for several years, allowing us to both save and invest. Building these habits and a nest egg was important to us as we approached parenthood.

Are your approaches to finances similar when it comes to planning for your family?

Mostly yes. We have areas where we disagree (such as public versus private hospitals and schools), but we talk about everything in depth and regularly have 'finance dates' where we assess the month prior and plan for the future. I tend to have a more conservative approach whereas Dion has more of the abundance mindset naturally. It's definitely a pro that we think differently because it often means we end up somewhere in the middle. We expect that our views will change throughout different life phases, but we try to keep our end goal in sight. Communicating regularly ensures that negative feelings don't build up and we approach changes with a clear head.

How have you and your partner budgeted for the cost of having a child?

We have created a separate high yield savings account for baby and birth expenses that we have contributed to monthly since we found out we were expecting (currently about $1000 a month, with additional top ups with quarterly bonuses). We have also increased contributions to our emergency fund. Once the main medical expenses are covered, we will use the leftover for more expensive items, such as a pram and a car seat. We are having a baby shower and have kept the registry focused on practical and affordable items based on the recommendations of other young families in our lives. We will be living out of suitcases as we will be travelling for most of the first year, so we don't want to lug around an overwhelming number of toys and onesies. We both love a bit of data, so we have a schedule for upcoming and anticipated expenses. We have mostly combined our finances.

What are some of the medical costs you considered?

I lost the argument on public versus private hospital, so we are going to have the bub in a private hospital. When searching for obstetricians, we found them to be very forthcoming about the costs to expect in advance as well as what Medicare covers. Understanding where private insurance chips in is more difficult – all of the documentation is very vague, so we have spent a lot of time on the phone with them digging into the details and always request a follow-up in writing, just in case! With our insurance limits resetting for the new year, we made sure to max out things like aids, appliances and prenatal care that we could front-load. While it's not posted anywhere in our insurance's terms and conditions, a note from our obstetrician meant we could claim back up to 80% on a breast pump, birthing classes, recovery garments, tens machine and more. This money would have gone unused for the year otherwise and provided substantial savings.

You are planning to travel for six-plus months while on parental leave – fun! How are you financially planning for this?

Travel has been a huge part of both of our upbringings and we want to share that with our growing family, whether or not he will remember it! Because we both have decent parental leave, it's cost-efficient to travel with a baby and it's easier when they are not yet mobile, so we've decided to take advantage of this time and have cancelled our lease from December so we can put many of our standard living expenses towards travel.

Another key deciding factor is that neither of our families are based in Sydney – Dion is from the Gold Coast and I am from Denver. We want to be able to spend time with loved ones and to also have that extra bit of support, because we know we will need it! We plan to spend about three months each in the US and Europe.

What are your plans for parental leave?

Strangely, Dion has more paid parental leave than I do (26 weeks versus 20 weeks), but we are both very fortunate, especially in comparison to the standards in the US. The baby is due in September and we won't be heading overseas until December, so Dion will continue to work and will start his leave from then to help with cash flow. We will both end up taking some unpaid leave as we are looking to return in July, but we know this is a unique time when we don't have the responsibility of a mortgage, pets or other kids, so we are willing to take a bit of a hit for the time being.

One great perk from my work is that they offer a transitional ramp period on the way back to the office. After the 20 weeks plus unpaid leave is up, I can work one to four days a week for the first four weeks back and still receive full pay. I will begin this as we return to Australia in July 2024. Additionally, I can work ten days to 'keep in touch' during the unpaid leave. I intend to join planning and strategy days and team offsites, and to extend my ramp period.

How are you thinking about generational wealth for your child?

While we definitely want to leave an inheritance for our kids, it is also a key focus of ours to invest in them and for them while we are still around. Setting them up with a good education and minimal debt is important to us, as well as instilling a strong work ethic, independence and flexibility to build a lives of their own. Travelling and spending time with them (rather than working long hours into our 60s) will pay a different type of dividend.

Do you have any advice for anyone contemplating parenthood?

Every child entering the world deserves the best. Fortunately, 'the best' has little to do with income level and more about the family and community around them.

Table 3.7: Kaylie and Dion's pregnancy expenses

Item	Month	Up-front cost	Medicare or health rebate	Net cost
GP	January	$30.00	$0.00	$30.00
Ultrasound	January	$205.00	$53.10	$151.90
Obstetrician – intro visit	February	$300.00	$76.00	$224.00
Noninvasive prenatal testing (NIPT)	February	$480.00	$0.00	$480.00
GP for ultrasound referrals	March	$30.00	$0.00	$30.00
Week 20 ultrasound	April	$460.00	$88.45	$371.55
Obstetrician – week 28 visit	June	$5,500.00	$551.00	$4,949.00

Item	Month	Up-front cost	Medicare or health rebate	Net cost
Compression garments for post-birth	June	$201.00	$152.00	$49.00
Portable breast pump	June	$529.98	$416.00	$113.98
Birth class	July	$405.00	$150.00	$255.00
Baby shower	July	$600.00	$0.00	$600.00
Third-trimester ultrasound	August	$425.00	$88.45	$336.55
Pelvic physio	August	$300.00	$240.00	$60.00
Baby essentials	August	$5,000.00	Less baby shower gifts	$5,000.00
Hospital excess	September	$250.00	$0.00	$250.00
Hospital double suite package (food and accommodation)	September	$500.00	$450.00	$50.00
Anaesthetist/ epidural	September	$1,150.00	TBD	$1,150.00
Caesarean section	September	$1,150.00	TBD	$1,150.00
Paediatrician	October	$500.00	TBD	$500.00
Baby travel (passport, vaccinations, visas)	October	$1,000.00	N/A	$1,000.00
Total		$19,015.98	$2,265.00	$16,750.98

Chapter 4

Preparing for parental leave

'Your children need your presence more than your presents.'

Jesse Jackson

Parental leave is very personal. Each parent has a different idea of how much time they want to take off from work (if any!) to stay home and raise their kids. Some plan on a career break until the kiddos go to school, some want just enough time to adjust to the newest addition of the family, and some wish to return to work as soon as possible.

Many parents are limited in how much time they can take off due to financial pressures. With Australia having one of the least generous paid parental leave policies in the developing world, it's not surprising that juggling the costs and expectations is a struggle. On top of that, parental leave is still heavily skewed towards mothers, impacting their income, super and future prospects. This often reinforces the gendered stereotype that women are natural carers of small children. Having a more gender equal paid parental leave and a shared care duty between parents is better for mothers, fathers, children, and also the economy.

There are many suggestions as to why fathers are less likely to take parental leave, including a study by Circle In that found '72% of dads say it was their workplace culture or manager that stopped them from taking parental leave'. This is quite unfortunate, especially since fathers who participate more in child care duties and family life tend to have greater life satisfaction. The result of their involvement is that their children tend to have better emotional outcomes and physical health, and are smarter.

Furthermore, a 2022 study by the Workplace Gender Equality Agency (WGEA) found that while primary carer paid parental leave is becoming increasingly available to both men and women (as per the government's parental leave pay, PLP, which can be accessed by either parent), only 12% of those who take it are men. This is up from 1 in 20 Australian fathers taking primary carer duties in 2019, but it is still low by global standards. Fathers are more likely to identify as secondary carers and take a shorter leave than their partner in most heterosexual relationships. Countries with older and well-established paternity leave policies have a greater take-up rate than those with more recently introduced policies. Unfortunately, policy isn't the only factor holding fathers back from taking leave – it takes a while for things to shift culturally as well. In comparison, research from Sweden found that same-sex couples shared parental leave more equitably than different-sex couples.

Navigating the social norms of parental leave can be challenging. Regardless of your personal situation, having flexibility and options is advantageous for any parent. That's why preparing financially for parental leave is an important first step.

The motherhood penalty and gender wage gap

Before diving into the topic of parental leave, it's important to acknowledge that parenthood affects mothers' and fathers' careers differently.

Mothers in the workforce experience additional disadvantages to women who are not mothers. Not only are mothers stereotyped as being less productive and competent, they are also more likely to receive worse financial compensation after becoming mothers. In fact, for every child a woman has, her income decreases by 5% to 20%, whereas men's incomes increase by about 6% when they become fathers. Apparently, men who enter fatherhood are seen as being more productive, motivated and financially responsible than prior to becoming a parent. Australian mothers, on the other hand, stand to earn $2 million less over their lifetime than fathers.

Talk about double standards! This phenomenon is referred to as the 'motherhood penalty' and the 'fatherhood bonus'.

Historically, roles typically occupied by women have been thankless and underappreciated (thanks patriarchy!). This extends from child care to the workforce, where 23 of the 30 lowest-paying jobs – including food service, housekeeping and ECEC work – are dominated by women (I rant about this in chapter 5), whereas 26 of 30 highest paying jobs are dominated by men.

Some might argue that women should negotiate better or ask for promotions and raises. The truth is that women do ask, and some-times more effectively than their male counterparts. Unfortunately, women who negotiate anticipate receiving backlash – and rightfully so, as one study suggests that women are more likely to be penalised when negotiating.

Furthermore, once large numbers of women join industries dominated by men, wages in those industries decrease regardless of education, work experience, race and geography. And since we are on the topic of wages, in 2023 the Australian Bureau of Statistics released a report stating that for every $1 men make on average, Australian women earn 87 cents. The average full-time working woman earns a base salary of $1653.60 per week, while the average full-time working man earns $1907.10, meaning women earn a total of $253.50 less than men every week due to their gender. That's $13,182 a year!

As though the gender pay gap isn't depressing enough, having it compounded with the motherhood penalty means that becoming a mother can negatively impact your earning potential.

Now, without getting into the politics of dismantling the patriarchy, let's prepare the best we can for parental leave in order to mitigate any financial stress and ensure you and your family are well equipped.

Planning for taking parental leave

'Parental leave sounds great,' a childless colleague told me a few weeks before I took parental leave for my first pregnancy. 'You have all this free time to take on new hobbies and try new things. What do you think you'll get up to?'

'Uh,' I paused, not knowing how to respond. 'I think I'm just going to try to adjust to looking after a small human.'

Parental leave is unique to each parent. For some it's about survival and finding any free time to nap and try to stay sane. Others fully embrace parenthood by trying to recreate sensory activities they saw on Instagram. And some, such as myself, attempt to balance parenting life with a side passion project to hold onto any semblance of an identity outside of being a carer. (By the way, 76% of parents believe the biggest identity shift happens when they become parents, and I tend to agree!)

Whatever your situation is, you may find that you are sometimes at the mercy of your baby. Balancing colic, sleep windows and researching the best baby food recipes, parental leave is full of unexpected surprises. It's true what they say: the days are long but the years are short. Never in my life have I felt like time stood so still while also passing at a blink of an eye.

Whatever you do choose to do, it is a good idea to plan for parental leave and consider your personal, financial and professional goals during this time. Being proactive about your expectations can make the transition into parenthood and back to work as smooth as possible.

Here's a checklist of what you may need to consider while planning leave:

- **Know your leave timeframe.** Will it be short or long? Will you be the only one taking leave or sharing leave with a partner?
- **Understand any paid/unpaid parental leave you (and/or your partner) may be entitled to.** Are you or your partner entitled to a government subsidy? Is your employer providing you with any paid or unpaid leave? Is your employer paying any super?
- **Coordinate leave with your employer and your partner (if you have one).** Does your employer have any expectations? Will you and your partner take leave at the same time or not?
- **Calculate your financial needs and expenses during leave.** Will you be able to cover your expenses while on leave? Will you need additional money (such as savings) to achieve your desired leave timeframe? Will you need an alternative income source?
- **Plan for your return to work.** Will you return to work gradually or full time? Do you need any support from your employer during your return to work? Will you be able to align your ECEC days with your work schedule?

What parental leave are you entitled to?

To be more inclusive, I prefer to use the term 'parental leave' over maternity or paternity leave; however, if I need to differentiate between the terms, I will. Also, while this information is accurate at time of writing, government parental leave pay entitlements do change from time to time, so please visit the Australian government website for the most up-to-date information.

In Australia, you are eligible to take parental leave when:

- you give birth
- your partner gives birth
- you adopt a child aged 16 or under.

Most companies offer maternity or primary carer leave – and paternity or secondary carer leave is becoming increasingly common – but this leave is often unpaid. (Employer-paid leave is covered later in this chapter.) However, in some cases you and your partner may be eligible for the Australian government Parental Leave Pay (PLP) scheme and other paid schemes (which I cover in detail later in this chapter).

If you're a permanent full-time, part-time or even casual employee, you are entitled to 12 months of unpaid parental leave from the expected date of your child's birth or when you start caring for your adopted child. (Those who are planning to adopt are also entitled to take two weeks of unpaid pre-adoption leave.) If you need more time, you can ask your employer to grant you up to another 12 months, totalling two years of leave. To be eligible for this leave, you need to have worked for your employer for at least 12 months and be the primary carer.

You're required to provide written notice to your employer at least 10 weeks in advance of taking parental leave and provide them with your expected leave dates. Often it's fine to adjust your dates as timelines shift, especially if your return-to-work date changes.

During parental leave, you are also able to take paid leave such as annual leave and long-service leave, which can provide additional income while on leave.

If you've previously taken parental leave, you don't have to work another 12 months before taking another period of leave with the same employer. However, if you have started a job with a new employer since taking parental leave, you need to work there for at least 12 months before being entitled to parental leave.

It's illegal for your employer to discriminate against you on various grounds, including leave entitlements, pregnancy, breastfeeding and family responsibilities. So, if your employer is giving you a hard time, know that you have the law on your side!

Keeping in touch days

If you'd like to stay connected to your role and organisation, and keep your skills fresh, you are entitled to ten keeping in touch days. You can use these days to stay informed through planning, attending a conference or doing training.

The keeping in touch days should not affect your unpaid parental leave entitlement and can be taken at least 42 days after the birth or adoption. They are not required if you don't wish to take them.

The payment for keeping in touch days is as per your normal wage. Leave is accrued for the keeping in touch days worked.

Government Parental Leave Pay

Your family may be eligible for the Australian government PLP scheme if you have a newborn or newly adopted child. Please keep in mind, some of these figures may change due to indexing or policy adjustments, so be sure to check the government website for accurate information.

At the time of writing, your family can get up to 100 days of PLP or 20 weeks at the national minimum wage. That amounts to $162.49 a day before tax (yes, PLP can be taxed) or $812.45 per five-day week. The total 20-week PLP that you'd be eligible to receive would be $16,249. The government has committed to increasing the scheme to 26 weeks by 2026, which is exciting. Please note that if you are coupled, PLP can be shared. The most one parent can take is 90 days, which is 18 weeks. (Single parents are able to take the full 100 days of PLP.) Parents can decide to take up to 10 days of PLP at the same time. This system is designed so parents can share caring responsibilities. PLP is also available to those who have made an adoption plan for their child or are part of a surrogacy, as well as those who have had a stillborn child.

To receive PLP, you must:

- care for a newly born or adopted child
- meet the income test

- not be working during your PLP (except for allowable reasons – check with the ATO)
- have met the criteria for the work test
- have registered or applied to register your child's birth with the birth registry.

In most cases the government makes PLP payments directly to your employer, but you do however need to fill out the necessary paperwork via Centrelink. This isn't to be confused with your organisations' parental leave pay, provided they offer it. (I'll get into more detail about that shortly.)

If you are self-employed you must not work on any days you receive PLP.

Income test

In order to assess your eligibility for the PLP, the government verifies your adjusted taxable income. To pass the individual income test, you need to have an income of $168,865 or less (as of the 2022-23 financial year) in the financial year before the birth or adoption, or before the date you lodged your claim (whichever date is earlier).

Now, if you don't meet the individual income test but are partnered, you can use the family income test. You're eligible to receive PLP if your family income is no more than $350,000 in a financial year.

Work test

The work test is a requirement to claim PLP. If you're the birth mother or first adoptive parent, you need to meet the work test requirements. If you are not the birth mother or first adoptive parent, then you and the birth mother or first adoptive parent must both meet the test requirements.

The work test requires that you have worked for 10 of the 13 months before the birth or adoption of your child and a minimum of 330 hours (around one day a week) in that period.

If you are self employed, and are undertaking paid work for financial reward or gain (even if the business isn't currently profitable), you may be able to meet the work test requirements.

It can be challenging to fulfill the requirements of the work test for those who have births close together or are in poverty.

How to claim PLP

You can claim PLP up to three months before the birth or adoption of your child, but the payments will only begin once you have provided all necessary documents, including proof of birth or adoption.

To make a claim, speak to your employer about your intention to receive PLP. They will coordinate the payment, and they will need to register with the government to do so.

You will also need to ensure that you know how many days of PLP you and your partner intend to claim, then log into Centrelink through MyGov to make the claim. On MyGov you will be able to track your claim and any additional information (such as the Child Care Subsidy, which I'll discuss in chapter 5).

Other benefits and subsidies

I'm not going to go into all of the various benefits and subsidies the government has on offer, but I will name a few in case they are helpful in your situation. All of these can be found on the Services Australia website. Most of these benefits require you to meet certain criteria in order to be eligible (such as an income test, resident rules or even vaccination requirements).

The **Family Tax Benefit (FTB)** is a two-part benefit that can help with the cost of raising children. The amount you receive depends on your specific situation and various criteria. Eligibility is also divided into two parts, so it is worth looking into it on the Services Australia website to see if you qualify. You can apply for the FTB at the same time you apply for PLP.

Under the FTB Part A you may be eligible for additional payments including:

- The Newborn Upfront Payment and Newborn Supplement
- Multiple Birth Allowance (please note, ironically the government doesn't consider twins as multiple births, only triplets and upwards of multiples)
- Rent Assistance
- A Health Care Card.

If you're a single parent, a non-parent carer, a grandparent carer or a member of a couple with one main income, you may be eligible for additional support under FTB Part B.

Some other benefits and subsidies include the following:

- **Child Care Subsidy (CCS)** and **Additional Child Care Subsidy** assist with the cost of early childhood education and care. (I go into greater detail about this subsidy in chapter 5.)
- **Parenting Payment** This is the main income support payment while you're the main carer of a young child.
- **Single Income Family Supplement** This is an annual payment of up to $300 for eligible families.
- **Stillborn Baby Payment** is a one-off, non-taxable payment your family may be eligible for in the case of a stillbirth.

Employer-paid parental leave and superannuation

Employer-funded paid leave is becoming increasingly common. In 2020–21, the Workplace Gender Equality Agency (WGEA) found employers that offered paid leave on average offered ten weeks for primary carer's leave and two weeks for secondary carer's leave. Now, not all employers offer paid parental leave, but according to the WGEA, three in five employers (60%) offer some type of parental leave (either to both carers or only to women). This is on top of the government PLP scheme.

Before you start planning your parental leave, it's advantageous to check your employer's parental leave policy to determine your eligibility and how much leave you're entitled to. Of course, in Australia, you're entitled to a year of unpaid leave, but your employer may have a more generous leave policy (or they may not).

This may be tricky to navigate in the early months, especially if you haven't told anyone you're expecting. But gaining clarity around what your employer offers is an important part of planning your leave and finances.

Keep in mind that prior to taking leave, you need to notify your employer in writing at least ten weeks before your last day of work.

Some organisations have employee policies that outline leave entitlement. Some items you may want to look for include:

- what you're entitled to
- whether you get paid parental leave (sometimes this is pro-rata)
- whether you get paid superannuation
- whether you get paid leave for appointments
- the policy around keeping in touch days (discussed earlier in this chapter)
- whether there are any additional benefits (such as mental health plans)
- whether there is additional support for single parents
- your return-to-work entitlement.

Your employer needs to adhere to the policies outlined by Australia's Fair Work Ombudsman, although any benefits beyond that are at your organisation's discretion.

How to create a leave policy for your employer

Some employers may not have a parental leave policy – or it may be in dire need of a revamp – in which case you may want to provide some suggestions on how the policy can be improved.

The WGEA Employer of Choice for Gender Equality (EOCGE) citation suggests that employers provide a minimum of eight weeks of paid parental leave at full pay for primary carers and a minimum of three weeks for secondary carers. This is on top of the government's PLP scheme.

If you're attempting to implement a new leave policy at your work, you may want to present your employer with some suggestions of best practices. The WGEA has some great suggestions for doing so:

1. **Gather data** – Collect any data that your employer needs to make an informed assessment. This can include how many parental leave requests the company gets over a year, the amount of leave employees take and employee retention rates after leave.

2. **Build a case for paid leave** – Having a good paid parental leave policy is a great recruiting and retention tool for any organisation. Also, empowering parents – and particularly women – to return to the workforce increases an organisation's diversity of experience and knowledge and contributes to reducing the gender pay gap. Also, parents going on leave provide opportunities for other employees to take on new roles and upskill. (This happened to me when my colleague was on parental leave, allowing me to get promoted!) It also reduces the stigma around child care duties and provides opportunities for secondary carers – often fathers – to take on a more active role in caring for their kids.

3. **Present your findings to leadership** – One of the best ways to create change in an organisation is to find others who support your ideas and findings. Often the leadership team is interested in how policies can benefit the organisation. Therefore, if you can share any case studies and data, and outline any risks and (especially!) benefits, it can help to make the case for why paid parental leave is necessary and viable for your organisation.

4. **Consult with other employees** – Receiving others' feedback on what policies would benefit them is crucial in getting other

employees on board and ensuring that the policy created reflects the needs of people in your workspace.

5. **Create a policy** – Work with the Human Resources team (or, if there is none, perhaps a colleague who is also passionate about parental leave) to create a concise policy that is written in language that can be easily incorporated into the organisation's existing policies.

Now, creating a policy may be the last thing on your mind when planning for a child. However, like all good ideas, someone has to conceive of it at some point to make it happen. I often like to think that we are paving the way for others when we try to make difficult changes.

Financial considerations and tax planning while on parental leave

Even though future financial and tax planning is one of the last thoughts on most people's minds when expecting a child, it's still worth discussing. Parental leave and your income can affect many aspects of your future planning, such as eligibility for benefits and subsidies and whether you're eligible to get a mortgage or credit card.

Income considerations

Many of the government-funded benefits and subsidies, including PLP and CCS, are dependent on an income test that considers your income and your family's combined income. If you're a low-income earner, this probably won't affect your finances. The government indexes some Centrelink payments and income limits, so this information is subject to change. At time of writing, if you earn more than $168,865 or your family income is more than $350,000 in the financial year prior to obtaining these schemes, you may not be able to access the PLP.

Some things that may affect your income for the financial year include selling an investment property and selling shares, which may massively increase your income for the financial year.

The income threshold was much lower when I went on my second parental leave, so I wasn't able to access PLP or the CCS due to the forced selling of company shares I held at my previous employer, which substantially increased my income only for that financial year. Now, I know my case is unusual, but if you are planning on funding your parental leave by accessing investments or increasing your wage the year prior to your child being born or adopted, it is worth considering the impact this may have on your eligibility for benefits and subsidies.

Loan considerations

If you or your partner are considering taking an extended parental leave, chances are you will be on a reduced income (and in some cases no income). If you are planning on applying for a loan, such as a mortgage or a credit card, the banks may look at your parental leave unfavourably due to the perceived uncertainty of your return (even if you have a planned return-to-work date).

Financial institutions want to ensure that you'll be able to pay the loan back, which is why they ask you to disclose if your financial situation may change in the near future. Now, the bank may not be able to ask you directly if you're pregnant, as that may be seen as discriminatory, but it may be flagged by the bank if you won't be earning an income for some time. If you aren't able to service your loan while on parental leave, this can put you and your family in unnecessary financial distress. It is best to be upfront with your lender, since they can help you budget, and providing misleading information on a home loan can have serious consequences for any future lending.

Mortgage repayment pause

Now, if you do have a mortgage but the budget seems tight during parental leave, you can ask your lender to pause your payments. Repayment pauses usually happen during parental leave or travel and are often granted if you are ahead of your loan repayment schedule, which is a great example of why it may be advantageous to make extra payments into your loan!

The positive is that you can allocate some of your money to other needs when adjusting to parenthood, but the negative is that your interest continues to accrue. Therefore, pausing your mortgage repayments may seem like a temporary reprise, but over the long run you will end up paying more in interest than if you continued to pay it off (see table 4.1). Nonetheless, it is a strategy that may be worth considering if your budget is tight.

Table 4.1: the cost of pausing your mortgage

	No pause	During pause	After pause
Monthly repayments	$1910	$954.83	$1968 ($58 more)
Total interest paid	$287,478	$0	$295.280 ($7802 more)

Scenario is based on Westpac's pregnancy pause offer, which is 50% repayments for one year, based on a $400,000, 30-year loan at 4%. The scenario assumes the pause happens 18 months into the loan and does not factor in fees.

SOURCE: RATECITY

Superannuation while on leave and the super gender gap

If you're employed in Australia, you most likely know that your employer is required to pay you superannuation (also known as a retirement fund). Employers make compulsory contributions into super based on a percentage of your income. At the time of writing it's at 11%, and it is set to increase to 12% by July 2025.

Super is often overlooked when planning for parental leave, as it's something that often happens without much thought (especially if you aren't actively contributing to it). Since you can't access your retirement fund for a while and child costs are a tad more immediate, it's easy to disregard super.

The truth is that ignoring your super can have consequential effects on retirement, especially for women. Women over 55 are the most vulnerable to experiencing poverty and homelessness due to the compounding effects of lack of super, taking time out of the workforce to care for their family and working part-time. Let's not forget the gender pay gap as well.

In regards to super, this compounding effect is often referred to as the super gender gap: Australian women on average retire with 23 to 28% less super than men. In fact, one source states that women retire with $136,000 less in superannuation than men and will accumulate $151,000 below what is considered necessary for a comfortable retirement. As if that isn't bad enough, most super funds charge fees while you are on leave even though you aren't regularly contributing (although some have started waiving the fee), widening the divide.

A report released by Finder states that the average full-time working woman who takes one year of parental leave will lose $16,800 in super. If she then chooses to work a four-day week for two years (as many mothers do in the first few years of a bub's life) then, that figure increases to $39,500. Although super is bound to be affected in some regard if you or your partner take leave, there are some things expecting and new parents can do to increase their super. In fact, just being aware is the first step. If you look up a compound interest calculator online, you can plonk in your expected super numbers and see the compounding effect of what you'd miss out on during the time you take leave. Finances may be stretched thin during this time in your life, but planning ahead can really pay off in the long run (or very long run when we're talking about super).

Pre-tax contributions: Salary sacrifice

Pre-tax contributions are also known as personal deductible, salary sacrifice, salary packaging, or the payments specifically are called concessional contributions (confusing, I know). Salary sacrifice is an agreement with your employer where you sacrifice part of your pre-tax income and, in return, your employer invests that into your super. The reason this is lucrative is because salary sacrificing into your super is only taxed at 15%, which is lower than most people's marginal tax rate.

For example, let's say you earn $80,000 and salary sacrifice $10,000. You will only have to pay your marginal tax rate on $70,000, which at the time of writing is 32.5c for each dollar over $45,000 (plus the 2% Medicare levy), and the $10,000 you salary-sacrificed is taxed at only 15%. Essentially, you end up paying less tax on your income, and in turn your money is invested into your retirement savings.

By investing in your super, you are growing your retirement nest egg and looking out for your own future, ensuring you have a comfortable retirement and reducing financial stress for your family.

There are limits to this benefit, though: your total concessional contributions are capped at $27,500 each financial year. Concessional contributions include personal deductible salary sacrificing and any contributions your employer makes to your super. When your superannuation balance is less than $500,000, you can carry forward the unused contribution limit for up to 5 years.

Government super co-contribution

If you are a low-income earner, you may be eligible for a maximum contribution of $500 via the government super co-contribution scheme in order to boost your retirement savings. To receive this, you need to meet the eligibility requirements, including contributing $1000 into your super. The positive is that you don't have to apply for the scheme if you meet the requirements – the government will make the contribution directly into your nominated super fund account.

Spouse super contribution

Although the name isn't my favourite ('spouse' refers to married or de facto partners, so 'partner' is probably a bit more inclusive), the spouse super contribution provides the ability to pay money into your partner's super from your after-tax income. Your partner may be able to claim a tax offset of up to $540 on the $3000 they can contribute to your super if they earn $37,000 or less for the financial year. This is a great way to ensure your partner's retirement savings don't suffer while they're on parental leave.

Spouse super contribution splitting

If you want to equalise your super balance with your partner's, you could partake in contribution splitting, which is the ability to transfer a portion of your recent super contributions to your partner's account. This is only available once per financial year and is dependent on whether your super fund allows it. This isn't held to an income test, providing more freedom to split contributions and reduce the gender super gap.

Focusing on your career while on leave

Of course, caring duties take precedence when on leave. However, that doesn't mean you need to let your skills and expertise fall by the wayside (unless they aren't a priority for you, which is totally okay too!).

Your career

Since your career has the biggest potential to increase your income in the future, it may be advantageous to remain somewhat connected to your profession while on leave. Some ways to stay connected and keep your brain fresh include staying active on LinkedIn and maybe even taking one of their courses. Another option is to write about your experience and share it, reducing the stigma that carers are less ambitious. A study by McKinsey found that US mothers show a higher level of ambition at work than their female colleagues. So, if you're one of those mothers (or carers), share your experience as a focused professional and ambitious multitasking employee. Going to meetups or conferences may also be a good way to still feel inspired while balancing carer responsibilities.

Starting a business or side hustle

For some parents who are on leave, nothing sounds more repulsive than doing anything related to their day job. Many of these stay-at-home parents and carers turn to entrepreneurship so they can have control over their own schedule while supplementing income. In fact, research conducted by Shopify found that 60% of mothers are interested in entrepreneurship, but mainly in a part-time capacity (whereas fathers were more interested in supplementing their full-time income). For those with passion projects, parental leave is sometimes a good time to test the waters and see if you can monetise them. It doesn't have to be a full-on business – it can be as simple as a side hustle that you want to make more lucrative. It's estimated that one in three women-owned businesses is owned by a mother.

Returning to work

Returning to work can be emotional, euphoric or both. I was beyond excited to stimulate my brain but sad not to hang with my little human every day. Having a flexible return-to-work plan is helpful as it can allow you to adjust as needed.

When talking to your employer about returning to work, discussing flexible work arrangements may be advantageous to ensure you feel supported and not overextended. Many parents return to work in a part-time capacity and then slowly work their way up to full-time hours. Having clear expectations laid out prior to returning to work ensures best outcomes for both you and your employer. For example, it's impossible to do five days of work in a three-day week, so duties may need to be reduced or meetings opted out of. But ensuring you and your employer are on the same page will keep you from feeling resentful and exploited.

Also, check with your employer to ensure they have resumed your super contributions so you can meet your retirement goals. In fact, 20% of women missed out on receiving their entitled super payments due to unpaid employer super contributions amounting to $1.3 billion during the 2019-2020 financial year.

You'll most likely have a lot going on balancing parenthood and work, so just remember to be gentle on yourself as you return to work, and know it's okay to have all the feels. (I know I did!)

Actionable steps

- Create a parental leave plan for yourself and your partner (if you have one), including how much money is needed to fund your parental leave requirements.
- Work out if you will be receiving any paid leave from the government and your employer. This includes any keeping in touch days and super contributions.
- Jot down any financial planning or tax considerations you may need to investigate prior to or during leave.
- Work out how much super you may miss out on during your leave and action a plan to reduce your super gap when you can.
- If you're feeling up to it, explore some passive income ideas or do some courses to feel engaged in your career.
- Make a return to work plan to ensure you are supported during your transition to work.

Ashley

33 | partner (33), one child (6 months) |
Newcastle, NSW

How did you start to think about finances before starting a family?

Honestly, I didn't give it too much thought! We were planning to buy a house so had been saving toward this for quite some time. In my mind the real costs of a kid were going to come up as they got older, so I kind of thought we would figure it out as we went. (This is often my mentality.)

How did you and your partner approach planning financially for your family's future?

My partner tends to take my lead on a lot of things, which is great because I'm a bit anxious and controlling. We agreed that moving closer to family and buying our first home were priorities for this stage of our life, so we really focused on what we would need to do to make that happen. We're both pretty level-headed when it comes to spending, and we're regularly checking in to make sure we feel like we're on track and happy with the direction we're going in. With constant rate rises since the birth of our baby, we're having these convos a lot!

How did you navigate parental leave?

At the time I was long tenured at my job, so I knew I would have access to some good leave to help me take a year off work. I made sure I was across all of these details as soon as I fell pregnant. My plan included a paid parental leave policy from my employer as well as long-service and other accrued leave. I was also eligible to access government leave, essentially ensuring that I could be bringing in around half of my salary for 12 months. I ran lots of scenarios in spreadsheets to try and make sure this would work for us. However, aside from two weeks leave, my partner had to remain working for this entire period.

When it came to thinking about return to work, I was a little less sure. I was hoping living closer to my family would mean reduced or even no childcare costs, although I knew having a mortgage would also make finances challenging. I was hoping to return to work part-time after my kids first birthday, depending on how our finances were looking. It was important to me to spend the first year at home, so we adjusted spending and life to achieve this.

You were made redundant while on parental leave; how did you navigate this situation?

So stressful! Although looking at it now this was probably the best outcome for me. Thankfully, with almost 10 years' service, my redundancy ended up giving us an unexpected cash injection – although I still need to find a new job! The redundancy has given me room to breathe. I will be able to take 12 months off work as planned, and possibly even longer.

We put my payout on our home loan with the option to redraw. We may use some of these funds for home renovations or to fund an extra few months off work, but right now it's lowering our interest, which is by far the biggest expense we have!

For any parents who are made redundant during parental leave, do you have any advice for them?

I think it's okay and important to grieve what you're losing. I found it really challenging to wrap my head around this sudden change, especially while I was so tired and emotional in the postpartum stage. I was sad and worried. But once I worked through these feelings and set out a plan for the immediate future, I felt much better.

My advice would be to take stock of finances and reassess your immediate goals to ensure you can find alignment between the two. Lean on your partner and support systems, and be kind to yourself.

How has having children changed your family's financial goals and lifestyle?

Life is a lot slower for me now. Nights out at wine bars and late-night Ubers home have been replaced with morning walks and peek-a-boo on the rug. Sometimes it's wonderful and sometimes I miss the freedom from before – it fluctuates! Financially, our goals are similar: pay down debt, resume some small investing, earn enough to enjoy a simple life. Honestly, at this stage the mortgage has changed day-to-day life more than the kid.

What are some of the financial strategies you are considering for your family?

We'd like to start investing a small amount for our kid and teaching them about money from a young age. Our parents taught us to work hard but didn't have much financial literacy themselves to pass on, so I'd like to set our kid up with a bit more understanding then we had.

We may need to look into side hustles or second jobs out of necessity. It's tough out there right now and life is only going to get more expensive as this kiddo grows.

Is there anything you wish you knew prior to having kids?

I know child care is going to be a big cost so I'm trying to learn as much as I can before that time comes. For this first year of life I think understanding that babies need very little has been really important. People will tell you about all the products you 'need' but they really only need the basics. So long as you can be present and attentive, that's really all they need.

What was the best piece of advice you've received regarding parenthood?

Surrender to it! You can't control this tiny human – you just have to go with the flow, forget your expectations and surrender to parenthood. It's tough, but the moments of immense joy really do make it feel worthwhile.

Patti

35 | Partner Joseph (33), one child (Zali, 2) | Brisbane, Qld

What was the biggest financial challenge you navigated as a parent?

No one really tells you about all the costs of having kids. I know I hadn't given it much thought until about a week before Zali was born. I put together a budget and ran the numbers, and was surprised to see that the cost of daycare in Sydney was on par with our rent. I couldn't afford not to return to work; however, half of my income would go to daycare fees. We knew that if we stayed in Sydney, we wouldn't be able to afford to have more children. The daycare fees were like birth control.

How did you navigate the costs of ECEC?

I had family in Queensland and knew Brisbane was a low-cost-of-living city, especially when it came to daycare and rent. I researched quality childcare centres and where my partner and I thought it would be best to raise a family, and we made arrangements with our employers to move states.

We managed to save $14,000 per year in daycare fees by making the move to Brisbane. This will free up some cash flow and allow us to pay off our mortgage faster. We basically halved our living expenses and our pace of life is much more relaxed, allowing us to enjoy our lives and give Zali more opportunities.

How are you considering investing in your superannuation?

I wish someone spoke to my mother's group about this issue since most new parents aren't thinking about their retirement when they are in the throes of raising a newborn. I never once considered the implications of taking time off for maternity leave and how it would have a huge impact on my retirement fund.

While on leave during the pandemic, I saw my superannuation drop $10,000. This made me realise that taking parental leave was going to have a massive effect on the amount of superannuation I accumulated for retirement. On top of that, it would also impact my career growth and earning potential.

I am now actively investing (salary sacrificing) 10% pre-tax and 10% post-tax to boost my superannuation and avoid the super gender gap.

How did you navigate returning to work?

I guess we always knew that our daughter would be at daycare as soon as maternity leave ended as my partner and I are both very career-focused. We knew the real cost of living in a city like Sydney would require a two-income household, especially if we wanted to buy a home. I did feel that mum guilt when I first left my daughter at care at 11 months old to return to work full-time, but I am so grateful for her development.

What were some of the things you considered when purchasing a family home?

Purchasing our own home was a big-ticket item, and we were so grateful to purchase while our daughter is young as we wanted her to have a childhood home to make memories and grow in that was stable and secure (free from the ups and downs of renting, which is what we experienced in Sydney).

We had three criteria for our home: it had to be in a good school catchment, close to amenities (such as shops and public transport) and back onto or be near nature (the coast, parks or nature reserves). A bonus was if we could buy a house with the potential to add value.

Have you done any estate or life planning?

Having a will is important for us as a family and we have started the process. We have a plan for our daughter in terms of who would look after her if anything happens to us, down to where we would like her to go to school and how we want her to be raised.

How are you thinking about generational wealth for your child?

We started an investment portfolio for our daughter from the day she was born and invest monthly so that eventually, when she is old enough and working, we can teach her the benefits of compound interest and the value of investing for the long term. Hopefully, the investment properties my partner and I have purchased will be passed down to our daughter so that she will not have issues buying a property when she is old enough.

How are you teaching your children about money and finances?

I started by teaching her the value in giving to others who are less fortunate. We volunteer at our local church, help others in need and give back to our local community through activities hosted by our local football community. We want to teach our daughter that investing in yourself and others is just as valuable as working hard for money.

Do you have any advice for new parents?

Budget, budget, budget. Agree with your partner first and foremost on what the budget looks like and try to keep to it. It may be foreign to you at first, but it definitely pays off when life is chaotic and you need a framework to keep some structure in your finances.

How do you budget your money?

Another tip (maybe controversial) my partner and I follow is that we keep our money separate. We have one central household account and we both pay into that at a 50/50 split. This covers food, bills, mortgages, house maintenance, our daughter's education and outings for us as a family. Outside of that, we invest our own money, and we manage our own insurances (health, car, etc.) and anything else.

Chapter 5

Navigating early childhood education and care

'Children having access to quality early education and care quite genuinely sets them up for lifelong improved health outcomes, social outcomes and educational outcomes.'

Georgie Dent

In a 2021 UNICEF study on the quality of child care in the world's richest countries, Australia was ranked 37 out of 41 on access to early childhood education and care (ECEC) and leave benefits, revealing the need for improvement to Australia's policies.

(Note: I use the term 'ECEC' throughout the book instead of 'child care' because I feel that it's a disservice to the work educators do to refer to their skills, expertise and knowledge as just 'care' – and don't even get me started on the dismal pay they receive! The education, support and learning outcomes they provide are absolutely invaluable to tiny humans. ECEC is actually our children's first experience of school. Language matters. These aren't babysitters; these are teachers providing our kids with the best opportunities possible. Okay, end rant!)

Unfortunately, access to ECEC isn't equal throughout the country. More than 9 million Australians live in areas where access to ECEC is insufficient. Those accessing regional or remote ECEC services are the worst affected, with a 2022 study finding that 50% of families in regional areas and 80% in remote areas are stranded without ECEC access. Research shows that those who would benefit most from high-quality education have the least access, and in many cases this is aligned with a lower socioeconomic status.

Australia is also one of the most expensive countries for ECEC, with households paying 31% of their combined income towards ECEC, while the world average is about 14.5%. (If your mortgage is about 30% of your income, there's not a lot of money left over!) Indeed, there's a lot more Australia can do to support parents and young children.

It's no joke that ECEC is expensive. It's one of the biggest (and most shocking) costs for new families, on par with housing costs. Although subsidies are available for parents that qualify, it doesn't take away from the fact that ECEC is unaffordable for many, and hard choices need to be made around whether a parent returns to work or stays home. In many cases, this choice predominantly affects mothers, as they are overwhelmingly the ones to take leave, or choose to seek part-time work to balance caregiving and work. Whether mothers predominantly take leave due to personal choice, societal expectations or finances, this disproportionately affects them and can have lasting effects on their careers, earning capacity and retirement.

Early childhood educators have a significant impact on young children's wellbeing, so it's paramount that there is investment in this sector. The sector has seen a high rate of turnover and burnout since the beginning of the pandemic, and educator jobs advertisements have doubled since the pandemic due to vacancies. It's no surprise educators are exiting in record numbers due to burnout, massive workloads, no career growth and, of course, low pay. Ranked the 13th-lowest-paid workers in Australia, early educators are highly skilled essential workers who are just looking for improved working conditions and fair wages. Having fewer educators means less access for families to the education and care their children deserve.

Why is this important, you ask? Because this is your child's education that's at stake, and this affects all families who have their children in ECEC. During the pandemic, some of these private centres made record profits – the sector turned over $14 billion, with 80% of the revenue from taxpayers. Some of these CEOs were paid millions all while receiving Jobkeeper payments, which were also funded by taxpayers.

Early childhood educators are integral to the quality of education our children receive, and their welfare affects every employer. If parents can't access suitable care, they can't work. If they can't work, they can't support their growing family. Ensuring that early educators are compensated adequately is part and parcel of building a thriving economy.

The truth is that parenthood, education and finances are all politically interwoven. It's our duty to build a world that our children can successfully thrive in.

Should you put your kid in ECEC?

I never went to ECEC when I was a kid. My parents' generation was full of stay-at-home mamas. At the time, it was both financially feasible and even socially expected to have one parent be the sole breadwinner supporting a family and paying all expenses, including a mortgage. But those times are far gone now.

Among my generation, as costs rise and incomes aren't managing to keep up, it's rare to hear of parents who are raising their kids without the support of either family or ECEC.

After my partner and I purchased our house, it would have been nearly impossible for us to keep up if I took five years off to raise children while my partner worked or vice versa. With the cost of living, the rise in inflation, the lack of grandparents and family as support and the impossibility of surviving on a single income, ECEC was our only option.

The other part is that when I did the maths, it didn't make sense for me to not work, not advance my career and not accrue super. Plus, by having both parents work, $36,400 of our household income would be part of the tax free threshold (since neither of us would have to pay tax on the first $18,200 earned as per the marginal tax rates), making it more advantageous for both parents to work. The flip side is that kids are only small once, need constant care, and that time is indeed precious. I know I've loved (almost) every moment I've spent looking after my children.

So, should you put your kid in ECEC? The reality is that there's no right or wrong answer – it's really up to everyone's individual circumstances whether to take on a full-time caregiver role or return to work or something in between. You know what's best for you and your family, just as my partner and I decided what was best for us. I took leave for the first year of each of my kiddos' lives, and I worked reduced and flexible hours when I did return to work. But everyone's circumstances are different.

Knowing what the costs of ECEC are and what you can afford is an important step forward in deciding what works for your family. Numbers are just one aspect to consider – the emotional side can often be a whole other topic.

Choosing an ECEC centre for your child

I had no clue what to look for at first when it came to the right ECEC centre for my child. To be honest, it was absolutely daunting. Feeling overwhelmed by guilt and various other emotions made the process so heavy. Know that you aren't alone if you feel the same way.

Types of ECEC

Many parents add their children to an ECEC service's waitlist early, even if they are unsure of when they want their child to start. In fact, some add their children even while they are still expecting.

Depending on your location and the type of care available to you, it may be worth considering early on what your child will need.

Here are some of the different types of ECEC services available:

- **Long day care** centres (also referred to as **early learning centres**) operate five days a week for at least eight hours.
- **Occasional/casual child care** is available for short periods of time.
- **Family day care** usually operates in the home of a registered carer.
- **Preschool** is available for children aged three to five prior to starting primary school.
- **Outside school hours care** is available before and after school, and sometimes during holidays.
- An **in-home carer** (also referred to as a **nanny** or **au pair**) cares for the child in their home.
- **Mobile care** is available for occasional care in rural and remote areas as they travel through.

It is important to check if the type of service you are looking for supports Child Care Subsidy payments, otherwise you may need to pay the full cost of the service. Some families use multiple services at the same time.

For a while I wasn't able to get my child into a long day care centre for all the days I required, so one day a week they were enrolled in occasional child care, which only operated from 9 a.m. until 2 p.m. – meaning I had to work a flexible schedule for that day.

There are also two main types of ECEC centres: community-owned (either run by a parent committee, a council or not-for-profit organisers) and privately owned (run by a company that reports to its shareholders). Although they may seem similar from the outside, research has shown that community-owned services provide better-quality education than for-profit companies. This isn't surprising, seeing as community-owned services are held accountable to their committees, which often comprise parents of the children attending and so focus more time and money on the children's development and wellbeing.

Privately owned centres, on the other hand, are beholden to their shareholders and focus on profit over quality of education. In fact, a 2021 study showed that for-profit centres are the biggest culprits of putting children at risk, comprising 77% of the 12,000 safety-breach enforcement actions against centres. That sits in stark contrast with community-owned centres, which outperform national averages for educator-to-child ratios (48% have more educators than legally required) and educators' level of education, ensuring that children get the support they need.

Considering ECEC fees

The financial strain that ECEC costs have on families is no joke, which is why the Treasurer directed the ACCC to conduct an inquiry into the ECEC services, fees and the CCS. The 2023 report by the ACCC states that the cost of ECEC fees have outpaced both inflation and wage growth over the past four years, rising by between 20% for centre-based ECEC and outside school hours care and 32% for in home care (see figure 5.1).

Figure 5.1: national average fees and out-of-pocket expenses, December quarter 2022

Centre-based day care	Family day care	Outside school hours care	In home care
$123.64	**$90.23**	**$30**	**$301.42**
Daily fee per child	Daily fee per child	Daily fee per child	Daily fee per child
▲20%	▲22%	▲20%	▲32%
Since Sept qtr 2018	Since Sept qtr 2018	Since Sept qtr 2018	Since Sept qtr 2018
$48.60	**$28.92**	**$13.54**	**$60.69**
Daily out-of-pocket expense per child	Daily out-of-pocket expense per child	Daily out-of-pocket expense per child	Daily out-of-pocket expense per family

SOURCE: ACCC

With the number of centres raising fees over the last few years, parents have to juggle multiple considerations, such as cost, quality, type of service and CCS. Although there are subsidies in place to lessen the burden and out-of-pocket expenses for parents, costs are still up 7% to 15.8%, depending on the type of ECEC, even after subsidy. There's a lot to consider when navigating this space, but we will get more into how the CCS works shortly.

What to consider in an ECEC service

Each ECEC service needs to adhere to the National Quality Framework (NQF), which is a set of guidelines set out by the Australian Children's Education and Care Quality Authority (ACECQA). The guidelines cover the required qualification of educators, the educator-to-child ratio and, of course, health and safety. Every ECEC service is graded and receives an NQF rating. These ratings can be looked up online to help you make an informed decision about the centres you are considering for your child.

While the rating is only one aspect of choosing a centre for your child, it's great to note that at the time of writing, 89% of ECEC centres received a 'Meeting' or 'Exceeding' national quality standards. Another important aspect is actually visiting the centre to see if it's a good fit for your child and family. Many centres provide tours and allow parents to come in for a play date with their child to see how they fit in.

Some things to look for when considering an ECEC service include:

- the centre's philosophy around education and care for children
- whether the educators are engaged and dedicated to providing a caring, nurturing and supportive environment for your child
- whether there is allocated time for play, learning and exploring new activities that are aligned with your child's development
- whether there is clear communication and expectations from both the centre and parents
- whether there is a lot of turnover of staff or a high rate of retention, providing stability for your child

- whether educator-to-child ratios are adhered to
- whether the centre runs all year or closes down during holidays
- how the service supports children with additional needs and requirements.

Visiting a few centres can provide you with a better understanding of what you are looking for and what your child's needs and preferences are. Remember, you know your child best, and if something doesn't feel right, trust your gut!

Debating your wage versus ECEC costs

Returning to work as a new parent can stir up a lot of emotions. I cried for a month in the lead-up to my return to work. I constantly questioned if I had made the right choice deciding to go back to work versus taking more time off to care for my child. During that time, COVID-19 was in full swing, there was a lot of job uncertainty and I needed to juggle the various aspects of my role as a parent and provider.

This can be a very conflicting time for new parents. In fact, some parents can't afford ECEC at all, or don't have access to suitable quality ECEC, making the choice even harder. In 2021, almost 140,000 Australians who wanted paid employment cited childcare as the main reason they couldn't look for work. Of this group, 90% were women. Among women out of the workforce who have children under the age of four, 82% state that domestic duties and ECEC as the reason they aren't doing paid work.

Weighing the decision can be hard. Just know you are making the best choice for your family with the information and resources on hand. The guilt can be a real, heavy feeling, but just remember – you are the best parent for your kid, they are truly lucky to have you and you are doing the right thing. There are, however, a few things you can consider when making your decision.

The cost of ECEC is a household expense, just like electricity, housing and groceries. It shouldn't be compared to just one person's income (especially the mother's, as it so often is!). It's a disservice to place the financial responsibility solely on one individual in a two-parent household, especially if it's a double-income household. Therefore, if anyone tells you 'my wage all goes to the cost of ECEC', remind them that it's a shared expense. This shift in language reduces society's bias in associating caregiving as the sole responsibility of one parent and instead emphasises that it's a shared venture.

Although ECEC is expensive, there are a lot of benefits to returning to work. It can provide an opportunity to have a sense of identity outside of parenting and improve mental health through connectivity with other colleagues. The financial gains can also be impactful as you continue to progress your career, upskilling or even taking on a new role (if you're career driven).

Plus, there's the compounding effect of superannuation. Often super is forgotten about when calculating wage versus ECEC costs as it's not cash in hand, but it can have a massive impact on your retirement. If you're a mother, let's not forget the impact of the motherhood penalty and the gender gap, and how those play into your career.

Kids who have access to ECEC greatly benefit from the experience. It's a chance for them to learn from educators, create lasting relationships and build social skills and trust. But more importantly, of the 300,000 children born in Australia each year, one in five start school developmentally vulnerable. For First Nations children, that portion doubles. Vulnerable children who start school without early intervention struggle to catch up to their peers and are more likely to have poorer life outcomes. With 90% of a child's brain development happening by age 5, exposing children to the supportive environment of ECEC can have improved health, social and educational outcomes. Plus, it's pretty awesome seeing little humans connecting with friends and coming home to tell you about their day.

It's worth acknowledging that there's a lot of guilt that comes with being a parent. Choosing to return to work shouldn't be part of that. You are doing the best you can for your family, and the choice you make is right for you. Plus, your child will love you regardless.

How does the Child Care Subsidy work?

The cost of ECEC varies across the country from $100 to $200 a day per child. This can be the equivalent of paying double rent or mortgage for many families (depending on how many days your child is enrolled). The government provides the CCS to assist with the cost of ECEC by reducing out-of-pocket expenses. It helps parents (especially mothers) participate in the workforce by reducing the financial burden of ECEC and encourages children to build new relationships, learn and develop through early learning.

Essentially, your CCS rate is calculated as a subsidised percentage of the cost of your ECEC fee. How much you can be subsidised depends on a few factors, including:

- your family income
- the type of care you use
- an activity test (determining the hours of recognised activities, such as work or study, that you and your partner do)
- the age and number of children in your care.

The amount you pay is the ECEC fee minus the CCS percentage you qualify for. This is also known as a gap fee. For example, if the ECEC fee is $150 and your CCS rate is 45%, your gap fee will be $82.50, and the remaining $67.50 will be covered by the CCS. The CCS is paid directly to the ECEC provider, therefore reducing the overall fees you pay to the centre.

To receive the CCS, you must:

- care for your child at least two nights per fortnight or have 14% of care
- use an approved ECEC service
- be responsible for paying ECEC fees
- meet residency requirements.

In addition, your child must meet immunisation requirements and must not be attending secondary school (or must be aged 13 or under, or 18 or under if they have a disability).

The CCS is applied for and managed through Centrelink via MyGov. The Services Australia website provides up-to-date information on the subsidy. The information in this chapter is accurate at the time of writing, but the government indexes some Centrelink payments to bring them in line with inflation, or introduces policy changes, therefore this information is subject to change.

There's also an Additional Child Care Subsidy for grandparents, those transitioning to work from income support payments, families experiencing temporary financial hardship and people caring for a child who is vulnerable or at risk of harm, abuse or neglect.

How much CCS can you get?

As previously stated, the amount you are subsidised depends on a few eligibility factors. Let's look at two of these – family income and hours of activity – in more detail.

Family income

In 2023, the CCS percentage and the family income limit were increased, allowing more families to access the subsidy. This incentivises more parents to enter the workforce.

For families earning up to $80,000 a year, the maximum subsidy they may receive is 90%. The income limit to receive the CCS is $530,000, which means that if you earn more than that, you will unfortunately not be eligible.

Your CCS rate is calculated on a sliding scale based on your family's estimated overall income for the financial year: for every $5000 your family earns above $80,000, the subsidy decreases by 1% (see table 5.1 overleaf).

Table 5.1: CCS rates from July 2023

Family income	CCS rate from July 2023
$70,000	90%
$80,000	90%
$90,000	88%
$100,000	86%
$120,000	82%
$140,000	78%
$160,000	74%
$180,000	70%
$200,000	66%
$220,000	62%
$240,000	58%
$260,000	54%
$280,000	50%
$300,000	46%
$350,000	36%
$400,000	26%
$450,000	16%
$500,000	6%
$530,000	0%

SOURCE: ONLY ABOUT CHILDREN

Usually, 5% of your subsidy is withheld to reduce the likelihood of an overpayment, which could result in a debt. This amount can be varied up to twice a year to suit your circumstance. Then, at the end of the financial year, your estimated income is balanced against your actual adjusted taxable income to ensure that you were subsidised the correct amount. This may mean that you need to pay back some of the subsidy (if you underestimated your income) or will be paid more (if you overestimated).

Calculate how much CCS you may be eligible for using the Child Care Subsidy Calculator at startingblocks.gov.au.

Activity test

In order to be eligible for the CCS, you need to do a recognised activity, which mainly falls under one of the following categories: work, training, studying or volunteering. Essentially, the fewer hours of recognised activity you are engaged in, the less CCS you will receive. Recognised activities include:

- paid work (including self-employment)
- paid or unpaid leave (including parental leave)
- unpaid work in a family business
- unpaid work experience or internship
- actively setting up a business
- doing an approved course
- training for work or employment prospects
- actively looking for work
- volunteering.

Your activity level is factored into your CCS rate calculation. If you have a partner, their activity level is also factored in.

The activity test restricts a lot of families from accessing CCS. In fact, a report from 2022 stated that 126,000 children from the poorest households are missing out on critical early childhood education and removing the activity test would have significant benefits, including greater early learning access for children of low-income families.

When the activity test was suspended during the pandemic, ECEC usage among First Nations children increased by 12%. This increase suggests that disadvantaged groups would benefit from eliminating the activity test. In 2023, the activity test was amended to provide

Aboriginal and Torres Strait Islander children with 36 hours of subsidised ECEC per fortnight regardless of the family's income or activity level.

CCS for more than one child

If you have more than one child under the age of five who requires ECEC services, you may be eligible for a higher subsidy. Usually, this means that the standard subsidy rate is applied to the older child, while the younger child (or children) may qualify for a higher rate – 30% on top of your rate up to a maximum of 95% as long as your family's combined income is under $354,305.

For example, if a family with two children under five has a combined income of $200,000 and they are eligible for CCS at a rate of 50%, the older child's CCS rate will be 50% and the younger child's rate will be 80%.

All this information can be accessed via the myGov website, connected to Centrelink. The steps are pretty straightforward, and the accompanying Services Australia website is full of helpful information.

Other considerations regarding CCS

There are a lot of other factors that affect your CCS eligibility. I had to navigate a few of them myself, from delayed immunisation reporting to being out of the country. Here are a few things that may be helpful to know when planning for your CCS.

Hours of care

The CCS is calculated by an hourly rate that is capped at $13.73, however, most ECEC centres charge a daily fee. The way this is calculated is the ECEC's hourly rate divided by the ECEC's daily fee by how many hours the ECEC is open for. This means that some families that opt for shorter hours, may in fact be paying more.

For a family earning $80,000 with a 90% subsidy, that attends an ECEC that charges $150 per day, there's a few different scenarios that can play out resulting in different payments (see figure 5.2). Here's an example:

ECEC centre 1: 90% of 12 hours @ 12.50 = subsidy of $135.00

ECEC centre 2: 90% of 9 hours @ 13.73 (capped rate) = subsidy of $111.21

Figure 5.2: how out-of-pocket-costs can change depending on how long your ECEC is open

This example is based on $150/day fee for a family with $80,000 household income and 90% subsidy.

SOURCE: ABC

The other thing to note is that the CCS uses ECECs' hours of operation for its calculations. So, it doesn't matter if your child attends for one hour or eight hours, the cost to you is the same.

When the activity test is also considered in the equation, things can get more complicated. For example, if an ECEC is open for 11.5 hours and a child attends five days (ten days a fortnight) the total hours per fortnight is 115 hours. If a family only receives 100 hours of CCS a fortnight (which is the maximum), then 15 hours a fortnight will not be covered by CCS and will be paid by the family. This means that a centre that is open for longer will use up more of your allocated hours.

Here's another example. If a family is approved for 75 hours, their child can attend eight days a fortnight at a centre that's open for nine hours. Alternatively, that same family can attend only six days at a centre that's open for 12 hours. The out of pocket fees can add up, depending on the operating hours of an ECEC centre. There are a lot of considerations when looking at the hours of care, including whether your child will need to attend for fewer longer days or more frequent shorter days (or a combination) and how many hours your family is approved for. The trade-off could be that if you opt for shorter days, you may end up paying more. They've made the system complicated, haven't they?

Absences

Your child is allowed 42 absences per financial year, which can be used for any reason, such as illness or holidays. You can track your absences online in case you are worried you may go over, which can sometimes be the case if your child has experienced medical complications or if your family has taken a longer holiday.

It's worth noting that CCS is generally not paid out if your child has any absences prior to their first day of physically attending an ECEC centre unless there's an approved reason. Instead, you will need to pay the full fees for the days missed. This means that if your child is enrolled in an ECEC service but your family is on holiday for the first two weeks that your child is to attend the service for the year, you may have to pay the full fees for those two weeks and the CCS will not be applied. This is also the case if your child is absent prior to their last scheduled day of enrolment at an ECEC service. For example, if your child misses the last week of being enrolled at their ECEC, you will also have to pay the full fees and may not receive the CCS for those days.

If your child hasn't attended an ECEC service for 14 weeks in a row, your enrolment with the ECEC service will end and you won't receive CCS for any absences after the last day your child physically attended the centre. This is worth noting if you are planning to take an extended holiday or there are any medical reasons your child is physically unable to attend an ECEC service for an extended time period. You may also stop being eligible for CCS if your child hasn't attended ECEC at least once in 26 consecutive weeks.

Leaving Australia

If you emigrate, your subsidy will stop when you depart.

If you're undertaking short-term travel, you will still need to pay for your ECEC service but may be eligible for CCS for up to six weeks. After six weeks, the subsidy will stop. This is just something to be mindful of while planning trips away.

Income planning

Since both paid parental leave and the CCS are based on income, it may be advantageous to consider any income that may impact your CCS percentage. Some families may think it's wise to sell property or shares or pick up a side hustle to help with the finances when taking leave or preparing for the cost of ECEC. However, any taxable income may affect your subsidy. It may be worth talking to a financial adviser or tax accountant who can help to ensure you receive the maximum entitlement while planning for any income changes.

Actionable steps

- Consider whether ECEC is right for your family by calculating the costs.
- Research a few centres in your area and compare their costs, NQF rating and proximity to your home. Schedule a time to visit them to see if they are a good fit for your child and your family.
- Jump on the Centrelink website and estimate your family's CCS to have an understanding of how much you could be eligible to receive provided you meet all the guidelines.

Bruce

34 | wife, one child (2), expecting number two | Gold Coast, Qld | name changed for privacy

How did you prepare yourself financially for parenthood?

To be honest, I never took personal finance too seriously until my daughter was born. I felt the desperate need to spend more time with her instead of working nine-to-five, so I started to educate myself by reading books and listening to podcasts relating to FIRE, property, etc. and started taking action towards financial independence.

How did you and your partner approach planning financially for your family's future?

My wife has been extremely supportive. We don't share the same level of frugality, but we have the right balance as we're very aware of how important it is to invest for the future but to also live in the present and create long life memories. We love to travel. I'm writing this from Corfu, Greece.

What was the biggest financial challenge you needed to navigate?

The major challenge was not financial – it was related to family support. Our daughter was born during the pandemic and we had to navigate the first few months of parenthood without support. As immigrants, this is by far the biggest challenge we face every day, to the point where we sometimes question whether we should go back home or not.

From a financial point of view, the one thing I regret the most is not starting to invest for the future before having my daughter. We would have been in a much better position, especially because there was more surplus cash to invest and let compound growth do its thing! The sooner you start, the better.

How did you navigate parental leave and ECEC?

We didn't want our daughter to be five days in daycare, firstly because it is too expensive, and secondly, and most importantly, we don't want our daughter to be raised by strangers.

As I have a higher income than my wife, it made sense for her to go part-time or casual. I think it's a great balance because my daughter gets to socialise with other babies and my wife keeps developing her career and building up her super.

We've decided to send our daughter an extra day to daycare, mainly because we have no family support in Australia. Our second baby is due in September, and we want to send our oldest to daycare three days a week before bub arrives. Those three days I will go to the office for work and my wife will only have one baby at home to take care of. When I work from home two days a week, I can support her when she has the two kids. Once maternity leave is over, both kids will go to daycare two or three days a week.

Financially, we will be in a better position when my wife starts receiving PLP from Centrelink, so sending one child to daycare three days a week won't affect us too much.

Have your finances changed with the expectation of your second child?

Not really. We'll just need to adjust our cashflow a little bit, but it shouldn't be too hectic – at least until both of them start daycare! Thankfully we don't have to buy a heap of baby stuff as we have most of it now. Just another car seat.

Have you done any estate or life planning?

We're in the process of getting our insurances and wills sorted. The most important things are to have basic needs covered (including education) and be debt free.

What are some of the financial strategies you are considering for your family?

We're investing in property and ETFs. I want to show my kids the value of money, the power of compound interest and the importance of investing for the future. We're planning to leave Australia in about 10 years, hopefully financially independent, and 'retire' in a cheaper country, possibly in South or Central America, or Europe.

Do you have any advice for new parents?

Nights will get better. Also, most of the baby stuff you see in the shops are wants, not needs. Their only need is you!

Jill

36 | partner Ben (36), twins Harvey and Eddie (6) | Brisbane, Qld

How did you start to think about finances before starting a family?

Ben and I were in a comfortable financial position when we decided to start trying to have kids. We had a small mortgage on a two-bedroom unit, and my employer had generous parental-leave provisions (14 weeks' full pay or 28 weeks' half pay, with super paid on the leave). I also had three months' annual leave and nine weeks' long-service leave stored, which would have enabled me to have eight or nine months off at full pay. We decided that we would stay in our unit for the first few years of bub's life before needing to upgrade. I drove a Suzuki Swift (fully paid off) and had no plans to upgrade.

What are your family's biggest financial challenges?

So, the first challenge was that it wasn't simple for us to get pregnant. After trying for six months with no success, I found out I had polycystic ovary syndrome and wasn't ovulating regularly. This meant specialist doctor's appointments, scans and additional tests and procedures. We were about to start looking at more invasive fertility treatments such as IVF when I fell pregnant.

Twins were a surprise and immediately came with additional costs. Firstly, my pregnancy was declared high-risk and so I was required to have private scans every few weeks at between $200 and $400 per scan. We couldn't fit two car seats into my Suzuki Swift and so needed to buy a bigger car. We also couldn't fit two cots into the second bedroom of our two-bedroom unit and so needed to upgrade to a property with three bedrooms. Lots of extra stress and trying to not buy a place 'emotionally' when you're six months pregnant was challenging.

I had to stop work at 28 weeks, which meant less time off work with my boys earthside. Then I got preeclampsia and they were born at 37 weeks. They were tiny and had no suck reflex, and so spent two weeks in special care nursery learning how to feed. I was discharged after five days, so my partner and I spent those two weeks driving back and forth from the hospital twice a day. It was exhausting and expensive, but because we had twins the hospital fed us both a meal (one parent fed per baby), which saved us from spending so much on eating out.

The government doesn't consider twins as a multiple birth when it comes to subsides. How did this impact your family?

I understand that twins are far more prevalent and it would make the scheme more expensive, but initial setup costs are way more with twins than single babies: two cots, a bigger pram, more clothes, longer hospital stays, and you're more likely to end up on bed rest during pregnancy. Even discounts to baby item providers would have been helpful.

I joined the local Australian Multiple Birth Association (AMBA) chapter, and they held a free expectant parent evening, which I found really useful. One benefit was that we got discounted baby formula, which saved us a lot of money. I tried to breastfeed, but my supply couldn't keep up with two hungry babies and we had to move to formula feeding. It did mean I started to get more than three hours sleep a night, though, which was nice.

How did you navigate parental leave?

As well as the paid leave I took, my workplace offered a program called Shared Care where if the primary carer came back to work full-time, they would pay their wage at 150% if their partner took unpaid leave and stayed at home with the baby. So, I went back to work full-time when the boys were six months old, and Ben took unpaid leave from work. If this scheme wasn't available, we couldn't have afforded for Ben to have that very precious time off with the boys.

How did you navigate the costs of ECEC and after-school care?

Childcare was next-level, with our childcare bills being almost double our mortgage repayments. Ben and I are incredibly fortunate to be on good wages, and I enjoy budgeting and forecasting our money, so I usually calculate our costs for the year, divide down by our pay cycles and put that much away in a separate account, with a bit of buffer in case of any unexpected expenses.

The year before our boys started school, we enrolled them in a kindergarten program. There was no rebate for kindergarten at the time, but it was cheaper than the daily rate at childcare. It did mean we had to juggle shorter hours on kindy days, which we managed by making up our work hours at night after the boys were asleep. We usually asked childcare for additional days around school holidays when the kindy closed.

Once they started primary school, I thought we'd see a big drop in childcare costs, but it wasn't as much as I'd thought. We were planning on putting the extra savings towards our mortgage, but instead they go to our boys' extracurricular activities.

How has having children changed your family's financial goals?

I definitely think about costs into the future more. I plan to send my boys to private school – unless they have a special interest that a local public school can cater to – and so I'm planning for that additional cost. At first I was concerned about the cost, but then I realised I would essentially be paying the same in school fees that we were in child care. That made me breathe a bit easier because we managed that okay, and our wages have gone up since then.

How are you thinking about generational wealth for your child?

We have investment bonds setup for each of the boys and one for ourselves. We plan to give these to them when they're 25 to help towards a house deposit or kickstart their own investing journeys. Ben and I were investing regularly last year, but with plans to renovate our house and interest rates being out of control, we've switched to putting the additional money back onto our mortgage.

Is there anything you wish you knew prior to having kids?

My two are currently going through the assessment process for ADHD and autism, and it's hugely expensive: $500 each for a speech assessment, $500 each for an occupational therapy assessment, $300 each for hearing tests and $650 each for a paediatrician appointment for diagnosis. And then it's $144 each for ongoing speech and occupational therapy each week. We have private health but are lucky to get back $100 total for each assessment and $70 total for each therapy session. Had we known more about what behaviour was considered age appropriate and what wasn't last year, while they were in prep, they would have received funding under the NDIS and costs would have been minimal, but because they've turned six we're not eligible for funding unless they receive a formal diagnosis. Even if we get a diagnosis, as expected later this year, there is no ongoing funding for ADHD as part of NDIS, so medical bills are expected to be a big chunk of our bills over the next 10 years.

Do you have any advice for new parents?

Make sure you have a solid emergency fund, because you never know when something you never even considered is going to pop up.

Chapter 6

Investing for your family's future: Investing explained

*'Someone's sitting in the shade today because
someone planted a tree a long time ago.'*

Warren Buffett

There are many reasons to invest for yourself or your child. It can provide security for your family, freedom to pursue other opportunities and improvement in your standard of living. Investing ultimately allows you to grow your wealth while you sleep, which is what makes it so impactful.

The other amazing part about investing is that it can provide a passive income stream through the distributions of dividends. Growing your income in this way can be a fantastic aid as you navigate the expenses of parenthood.

Investing can also help set up your child for success by funding their education costs, helping with a downpayment on their first home or just growing their wealth from allowances and birthday money.

Just over 70% of parents wish they had some help teaching their children about investing, so this chapter will provide you with a basic understanding of investing and confidence that you can draw on to make the right financial choices for your family. You're a financially savvy investor, remember? You've got this.

Whatever your reason for investing, it is a great first step in ensuring you are building wealth and securing your family's future.

You are investing right now

Did you know that you are probably investing right now? It's true – through your superannuation, which is a compulsory retirement investment account. It's the equivalent of a 401(k) in the USA, New Zealand's KiwiSaver or my former home country of Canada's Registered Retirement Savings Plan (RRSP). These governments recognise that investing for the long term can be a powerful step in growing wealth, which is why, through regular contributions and holding your investments for a long time, you have probably seen your balance grow over the years.

For many people, investing in their super may be the most advantageous way to invest, since pre-tax contributions are taxed at 15%. For most, this is lower than their marginal tax rate. It may be worth talking to a financial adviser to understand what option is best for you.

Another thing to note is that investing does come with risk and the potential to lose money, especially during market downturns. However, since 1971, the S&P 500 has returned an average of 7.58%, or 10.51% with reinvested dividends, meaning that despite market fluctuation and volatility, historically investing has trended positively over a longer period.

For example, the S&P 500, which is one of the most popular indexes (or indices – same thing) and tracks the top 500 US companies – has always recovered from a market downturn. It's recovered from the Great Depression, the 2008 global financial crisis and the more recent COVID-19 dip (see figure 6.1). Although there are risks to investing, buying and holding assets for a long time period allows the market to recover from shorter-term volatility, which is a natural part of the market cycle.

Figure 6.1: the long-term history of the S&P 500

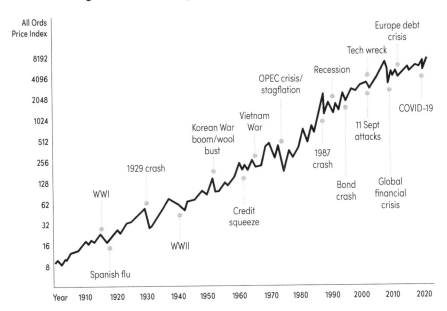

SOURCE: MORNINGSTAR

Another reason long-term investing is a popular strategy for many investors is that money compounds and grows the longer it's invested.

Working in the financial sector, one of the things I hear most often is, 'I wish I started investing earlier'. This is a common sentiment; in fact, I feel the same way. As the saying goes, 'The best time to plant a tree was 100 years ago; the second best time is now'. Now is as good a time as any to build your wealth.

Limiting investing beliefs

Many people think that the stock market and investing is reserved for white men in business suits yelling at giant screens of bar charts going up and down in a frenzy. Or, that investing is hard and you need a lot of money to get started. Or, my personal favourite, if you're bad at maths then you can't be a good investor.

Let me tell you, these are limiting beliefs. Investing is something anyone can learn and succeed in, even if you are terrible at maths! Long-term investing is more about behaviour and habit-building than anything else, which we discussed in Chapter 1. In fact, a 2013 study by Fidelity found that the best investors were either dead or inactive. Surely, if neglected portfolios and the dead can have strong returns, we can as well!

So, push away any thoughts of doubt. Investing can be a wealth-generating tool for you and your family.

The share market explained

Before we get into the logistics of investing, let's talk a little bit about what investing actually is.

We've all heard about investing in some form or another, whether it's property, crypto or finding the next hottest stock. To clarify, when I refer to investing in this book, I am talking about investing in low-cost diversified index funds on the stock exchange. Please note that the terms 'shares' and 'stocks' are often used interchangeably, but in Australia we usually use the term 'shares'.

Let's start from the beginning.

Shares are essentially divisions of ownership of a company, which means that by buying shares you are effectively buying part of a company. How cool is that?

Most people have heard of the share market (or stock exchange). Australia's is the Australian Securities Exchange (ASX). In the USA, there are two main exchanges: the New York Stock Exchange (NYSE) and Nasdaq. These exchanges are where people can buy and sell equities, such as shares of individual companies (such as Apple), bonds (fixed-interest investments), ETFs (exchange-traded funds) and REITs (real estate investment trusts). Many countries have their own stock exchanges that trade in their own currency, which you can access through a broker.

What's a broker?

If you can buy shoes online, I promise, you can buy shares.

I like to think of a broker as kind of like Amazon or eBay. A broker is a company or platform that facilitates the buying and selling of equities. To buy shares on the exchange, you need to use a broker. There are plenty of low-cost options available that allow you to access the ASX and the US stock exchanges to purchase shares or ETFs (which we will talk about more soon).

So, similar to Amazon or eBay, all you have to do is sign up, create a profile and verify your identity. Usually, you can put money into your account and purchase shares directly. All you do is click 'buy'. It's that simple. Seriously.

I often like to think, *Why buy shoes when you can own the company that makes them?*

Here are some things to consider when researching brokers:

- **Fees** – there are three main fees to consider when purchasing shares: transaction, foreign exchange and management fees. Transaction fees are fees that are paid every time you purchase or sell a share. Some platforms charge a percentage for larger transactions. Fees can eat into your returns, particularly if you are investing frequently, so finding a low-cost platform is advantageous. Foreign exchange fees (also known as FX) are paid when you transfer money to another currency. This usually happens if you are investing in international exchanges, such as the Nasdaq. Management fees are usually charged if you are investing through a micro account. There are also management fees of ETFs, which are deducted from the fund asset, which are separate to the actual broker fees. A broker's fee structure should be included in their product disclosure statement (PDS) on their website.

- **Your investing style** – some platforms are geared toward beginners while others focus on day trading. It may be helpful to find a platform that focuses on long-term investing and keeps you on course without tempting you to change your strategy. Having tools like goal setting, so you can track your progress, may also be useful.

· **Ease of use** – some platforms use a lot of investing jargon and are suited for those trying to time the market (also known as 'trading' or 'short-term investing'). It's worth checking out a few different platforms to see what you prefer and what investing experience works for you.

· **Automation** – if you are planning on investing regularly, having features that support your investing journey may be a plus. Much of investing is behavioural, so automating your investing can simplify your strategy while helping your investments grow faster.

· **Access to various exchanges** – if you want to invest directly in stock exchanges outside of Australia, it may be worth considering brokers that access other stock exchanges. There are, however, many ways to invest in different sectors and countries through the ASX that reduce tax implications.

· **CHESS-sponsored versus custodial versus micro investing** – if shares are CHESS (Clearing House Electronic Subregister System)–sponsored, it means that you have direct ownership of each share. Often the minimum to invest in a CHESS-sponsored product is $500. CHESS-sponsored shares are unique to Australia and are not an international model. Alternatively, some platforms use a custodial model, which means the assets are held on your behalf by a custodian (such as a financial institution). This may be beneficial if you want to access international markets, where there is no CHESS equivalent, or if you want to invest in fractional shares (or smaller amounts of money). Then there is micro investing, which is the ability to invest in units of a managed fund. This may be beneficial if you want to invest smaller amounts or use a 'rounding up' feature that allows you to invest a few dollars and cents every time you make a purchase.

There may be some analysis paralysis that comes with choosing the right broker, but know that you can always transfer to another broker (similar to swapping banks), so there is no need to get hung up on this – there's no single right answer. The best thing to do is just sign up to a few and see what works best for you.

Creating an investment strategy

The benefit of having an investing strategy is that it keeps you on track and focused on your long-term goals. It enables you to follow guides you've put in place. Here are some things to consider regarding your investment strategy:

- Determining your **risk tolerance** is an important part of creating an investment strategy that aligns with your financial goals. Your risk tolerance is your willingness to take on risk within an investment portfolio. (We will dive deeper into the risk factors of various investment types next.) When determining your risk tolerance, it is valuable to consider what proportion of your investments are defensive (more stable, such as cash, term deposits, fixed interest managed funds and bonds) versus growth assets that have a higher expected return (such as shares).

- It's important to consider your **asset allocation** – what assets you hold and what percentage you hold of each. We never know what asset class will perform well over the coming year, so ensuring your assets are diversified can mitigate some risk and volatility.

- **Diversification** considers what sectors, industries, and markets you're invested in. For example, it's worth asking if you are invested in one country and market, or across various ones such as the Australian, global, and the US equity market. What about sectors, such as technology, finance, commodities, and property? Diversification reduces your risk because different assets perform well at different times.

- Knowing your **timeline** is important for your investing strategy. Are you investing for yourself and an early retirement? Then your strategy may be different than if there's a distant horizon, such as investing for your child's future.

- Know you can always adjust your strategy as needed. In fact, whenever **personal circumstances** change, it may be worth re-looking at your strategy again and seeing if it's still applicable to you. Times when it may be valuable to reassess your strategy include when you experience a change in income, combining finances with a partner, buying a house, inheriting and, of course, having a baby. (Oh, and if you win the lottery – wishful thinking!) It is advantageous to wait at least six months after a big life event to make any decisions that may impact your finances.

By considering risk, asset allocation, diversification, timeline and personal circumstance, you can create an investing strategy that aligns with your and your family's goals.

Different types of investments

There are many different types of investments, each of which comes with its own expected risks and returns. Therefore, understanding your own risk tolerance is important in determining what asset classes you wish to invest in. Often, diversifying your investments can reduce risk, so it may be worth considering a few options.

Let's jump in and understand the different investment types.

Cash

Cash is often considered a safe investment as it's generally low risk (because it's very unlikely that you will lose cash). However, it's also low in returns, meaning it doesn't usually keep up with inflation. The benefit of holding cash is that it's a good option for shorter goals, such as saving for a holiday or for parental leave. It's also great to have cash for your emergency fund and if you need to pay down any debt. Due to it being low risk, it can also reduce volatility in your portfolio.

If you're trying to use cash to save money, a high-interest savings account may be ideal. If you have a mortgage, you may consider holding cash in your property offset account to offset any mortgage interest. The good news is that in Australia, the government's Financial Claims Scheme protects up to $250,000 per account holder should something happen to the banking system.

Regardless of where you keep your cash, it is one of the safer investments. You may not get rich off cash, but you most likely won't lose money quickly either.

Bonds

Bonds are a type of fixed-interest investment (the way that banks state what the interest rate is for their savings account). But where bonds differ from cash is that bonds are loans made to companies or governments (How interesting, right? You could be lending your money to the government!) So, like cash, you are likely to earn interest on your money, but unlike a savings account, bonds may go up and down, making them slightly riskier.

Usually, bonds have a higher return than cash, but there is a risk that the government or company you lent your money to doesn't pay you back. In more developed countries like Australia, this risk is very low as we have a fairly stable government, but there's always a risk. There is also the risk of bonds decreasing in value, which could happen if you invest in them at a low interest rate, but then interest rates steadily increase. Bonds are often used in a portfolio to reduce volatility alongside other riskier investments.

Property

It seems as though you can't talk about investing in Australia without mentioning property. It's one of the most popular investment types in the country, due in part to it being a more tangible asset.

There are various ways to invest in property. You can buy a tenanted rental property or commercial property and receive an income in the form of rent. Another option is to purchase REITs (real estate investment trusts) through the stock market and have the trusts invest in real estate for you. A third option is to invest in unlisted property trusts that allow you to have a share of the trust that owns industrial, office or health care properties that are rented to major corporations that produce income and can have a growth component.

Contrary to popular belief, property prices do fluctuate, but these fluctuations aren't as obvious as the stock market. In some cases property can also be seen as a liability, such as if it's built on land that's prone to flooding or fires.

The risk of investing in property is medium to high, as it depends on the type of dwelling, location and vacancy rate. Over the long term, the returns on property are expected to be higher than cash and bonds.

Shares

Shares (or stocks) are pieces of a company that you can directly or indirectly own. They are usually high risk, but the potential for return is also higher. Shares are often more volatile due to their constantly changing prices and the ability to buy and sell them easily (also known as 'liquidity').

There are two main ways to make money from shares: dividends and capital gains. I'll talk about these more later in this chapter, but essentially, dividends are when the company pays you (the shareholder) some of its profits (similar to receiving rent on property, it's the income payment from the shares), whereas capital gains are the difference in price between what the share was bought for and sold for, which is also similar to property capital gains. Dividends and capital gains are both taxable.

Exchange-traded funds (ETFs), which I'll talk about next, are bundles of shares that you can invest in, diversifying your exposure risk compared to owning shares in a single company. ETFs are best suited to people with a high risk tolerance and a longer time frame. The reason for this is that the market is volatile and a longer time frame allows the market to potentially recover from short-term fluctuation. Although shares are riskier than other investment types, they do have the potential for a higher return over the long run, which is why your superannuation is likely to be invested in shares and ETFs (see figure 6.2).

Figure 6.2: the expected risk and potential return of various investment classes

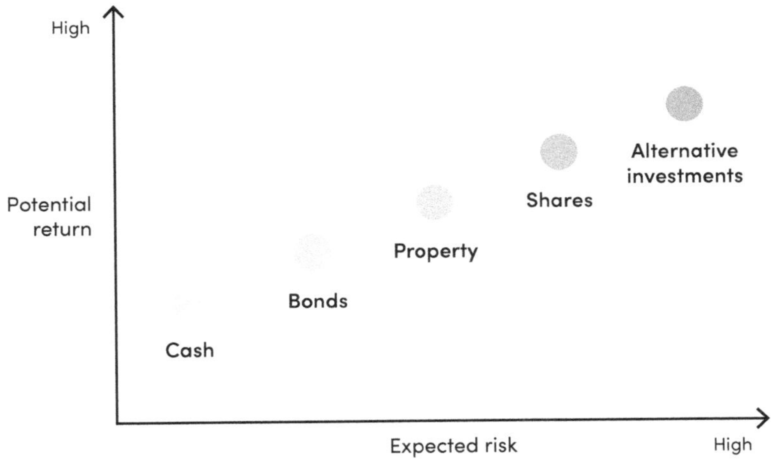

Alternative investments

There are also alternative investments that I won't discuss in detail but may be worth noting. Some alternative investments can be speculative, meaning they have a high degree of risk and uncertainty and can be quite volatile.

Alternative investments include cryptocurrency, non-fungible tokens (NFTs) and collectables (such as stamps, coins and LEGO).

These investments are not suitable for all investors and should be considered with caution as they can be very risky.

Low-cost diversified index funds and ETFs

When investing, it's considered advantageous to diversify your portfolio across multiple asset classes, sectors and countries to reduce volatility and risk.

Here in Australia, many people are heavily invested in property, which is kind of like putting all your eggs in one basket, since it involves investing a large amount of money in one asset class in one sector in one country. This is similar to purchasing shares in just one company. That one company may increase in value rapidly, but it could also underperform. Although all investments carry some level of risk, your overall risk can be reduced by diversifying your assets (which is like owning many types of properties in many different countries).

A really easy way to diversify your portfolio is to purchase an index fund that tracks the stock market. The ASX 200 is an index that tracks the 200 largest listed companies in Australia, whereas the S&P 500 tracks the 500 largest listed companies in the United States of America. Both of these indexes provide passive ways to track some of the largest companies in these markets across different sectors. However, they are focused only on their respective country's shares, which is why it can be advantageous to further diversify your portfolio across other indexes and countries.

ETFs are traded on the stock exchange and are composed of many individual companies. Some companies may perform well, while others may not, but since the ETF is tracking an index it will yield the average returns of the market. It's a passive way to ensure you are following the stock market as it grows (or dips).

By holding a whole bunch of companies, you are diversifying your portfolio and not having to guess which will perform well over time. Instead of having all your eggs in one basket, it's like having your eggs in all the baskets!

Some investors try to beat the market or opt for an actively managed fund that attempts to pick top-performing companies. Usually, these funds cost more in fees. In 2008, Warren Buffett, the world's most famous investor, challenged fund managers to a $1 million bet. Buffett believed that the S&P 500 could outperform the hand-picked portfolios of managed funds including the funds' fees. In the end, his passive investing strategy outperformed the active portfolios of professional investors, proving that investing in low-cost index funds and not tinkering with one's portfolio is generally a better option.

One thing to remember about investing is that prices can fluctuate depending on the economy, the performance of different companies, global events and various other factors. This is very normal and part of the economic cycle.

ETFs and the chocolate analogy

Investing in ETFs can be compared to a box of chocolates, which makes it both delicious and easy to understand.

The shares are the chocolates. You can buy individual ones, similar to how you can buy individual shares, but you won't know until you try them whether they are any good. However, if you purchase the whole box, you will get a variety of flavours, some of which will be hits and others less desirable. By having a diverse range, you can spread out the risk and increase your chances of a successful outcome. You may be surprised that the peanut butter-flavoured chocolate is the best, and you would never have tried it otherwise.

Similarly, a diverse ETF reduces risk as some companies perform better than others, and it takes the guesswork out of trying to choose which will perform best.

To continue with the chocolate analogy, you can purchase boxes of chocolates from a few different types of stores: supermarkets, confectionary stores or even your local neighbourhood corner store. These are like the different brokers you can choose from. They usually hold the same or similar shares, but they may have different costs and fees.

However, it doesn't really matter where you buy your box of chocolates, as long as it's low-cost and you've done your due diligence to diversify in order to reduce risk.

How do you make money from investing?

There are several ways to make money with investing, which is why it can be so powerful. There's also some tax planning that may also be required when investing.

Capital gains

When you invest in shares, the market will often fluctuate. For example, you may have bought a share or ETF for $60, but over time that price may have increased to $80, meaning you have earned a capital gain of $20 when you sell that asset.

Often this is the main focus in the media – whether assets have gone up or down in value. The truth is that unless you sell that asset, you have not realised the gain or loss. This is because you still own the same number of shares, it's just that their value has changed.

It's completely normal for the market to fluctuate, and in fact it's sometimes good to ignore your investments as they move up and down over time. It's only when you sell assets that you officially 'lose' or 'gain' money.

It's kind of like if you buy canned beans at the store for $1.50, and then the following week they are on sale for $0.85. You haven't lost anything, because you still have the same number of canned beans at home (unless you ate them) – it's just that now they are worth a tad less. But if you wait a bit longer, those same canned beans will most likely be worth $1.50 again, or maybe even more!

Just remember, capital gains are subject to taxes. In Australia, there is a capital gains tax discount of 50% on assets owned for 12 months or more. Tax is then paid on this assessable capital gain at your relevant marginal tax rate (unless your total taxable income is less than $18,200). This means that long-term investing may also be advantageous from a tax perspective, as those who hold their assets for longer than a year pay only half the net capital gain. Another win for long-term investing!

Dividends

The second way to make money from investing is through dividends.

When a company earns a profit, it can either reinvest the money back into the business or distribute some of the earnings to its shareholders in the form of dividends. Dividends are usually paid quarterly or annually in the form of cash or additional shares, which can be reinvested.

The benefit of dividends is that they are passive, meaning you earn money while you sleep. By simply holding onto shares, money will be paid to you, kind of like receiving income on a rental property. It's another magical part of investing!

Some investors focus on the share price when investing as it fluctuates, but it's valuable to also consider dividend income as this shows the true overall value of how a share or ETF is performing.

It is important to note that the total capital return of a share or ETF includes both the share price and the dividend yield. Looking at one part of the return (such as just the price) doesn't provide the whole picture of the performance of the investment. Some platforms allow you to track this for free, so there is no need to pull out an Excel spreadsheet for this.

Since dividends are a source of income, they are generally subject to income tax and are worth considering as a part of your marginal tax bracket (just like capital gains).

Franking credits

In Australia, there's this wonderful thing called 'franking credits', which are tax credits that are attached to dividends paid by Australian companies. These credits represent the tax the company has already paid on its profits before distributing them as dividends to shareholders. This is uniquely Australian as it only applies to Australian companies and Australian shares.

Under Australia's dividend system, shareholders can use these franking credits to offset the amount of tax they owe on the dividends they receive. If the franking credits exceed the shareholder's tax liability, the shareholder can receive a refund for the difference.

Taxation laws can be complex, so it's always a good idea to seek professional advice from a qualified tax accountant or financial adviser to ensure you're meeting your tax obligations and taking advantage of any tax benefits that may be available to you.

Actionable steps

- Take a look at what your super fund is invested in and the asset allocation. Take note of how it is diversified and if it aligns with your risk tolerance. Consider how you would invest similarly or differently outside your super.
- Think about your own investment strategy and how you balance risk, asset allocation, diversification, timeline and personal circumstance. This will help you stay on track as you invest outside of your super.
- Take note of the different types of investments you hold. Do you hold too much of one investment type or are you diversified across assets?
- If you are ready to start investing, sign up with a broker and make your first investment with your family's future in mind.

Brendan

40 | wife, one child (3) | Sydney, NSW

How did you first learn about investing?

I wasn't always interested in investing. I was lucky enough to meet someone who explained to me that they were making more money outside of work than they were making at work.

What was the biggest financial challenge you needed to navigate?

We had not started investing when we first had our son. My wife had almost 12 months off work; then, within eight months of her returning to work full-time, we had paid off two car loans, a credit card (only with a $2000 limit) and found a way to buy an investment property.

How did you navigate parental leave and ECEC?

We were lucky because during my wife's maternity leave, her work paid 50% of her salary.

We booked our son into daycare, and we were lucky enough to have my mum around the corner to drop him off there in the morning if needed. He is no longer in daycare and my mum now looks after him five days a week.

How has having children changed your family's financial goals?

Having a child was a big reason that we started to invest. We realised that the best way for us to ensure a great future for him as well as us was to invest.

Have you done any estate or life planning?

We do have insurance. Although we have spoken about getting a will, I hate to admit we haven't done it. (Crazy, I know.)

How are you planning for your family's financial future?

Our main goal is to spend more time together as a family as our son grows up. I do regret not doing investing earlier but that can't be changed. I recently changed jobs, and the times that I work have allowed me to start a side business that after only a few months has been able to net me about half of my salary at my current job.

Is there anything you wish you knew prior to having kids?

Go hard for years before having children. The costs are higher when you have them, so it's much harder to find money to invest.

Do you have any advice for new parents?

Invest with them in mind. Remember that eventually it'll go to them.

What was the best piece of advice you've received regarding parenthood?

That it's going to be fine.

Kim

38 | partner Teresa, one child (Grayson, 2) |
Melbourne, Vic.

How did you start to think about finances before starting a family?

Before getting married in 2019 we hadn't looked at our finances as a couple, despite being together for about seven years at that time. Planning the wedding and talks of starting a family made me want to look at our finances a lot closer, and I created a DIY budget on Excel with everything we spent on utilities, subscriptions, loans, insurance, transportation and food. This gave us the understanding of what our disposable income and saving abilities were, and also how long it might take for us to save to start a family through IVF or intracytoplasmic sperm injection (ICSI).

Fertility clinic websites were very useful as they often outline the potential costs of the whole process. After going over this together, we decided $50,000 was our limit. Next was to decide who was going to get pregnant. Teresa was a contractor at the time and wouldn't have been entitled to maternity leave payments, and I had been with my company for over 10 years as a full-time employee. Teresa was also earning more money than me. This weighed heavily on our decision for me to try first. We ended up spending $21,900 out of pocket (about $37,400 initially paid and $15,500 back through subsidies and insurance rebates) with three attempts before getting pregnant – and we consider ourselves very lucky.

What are your family's biggest financial challenges?

What a surprise as I was going through the process of getting pregnant and COVID-19 hit, and I was made redundant in March 2020. This was definitely not the initial plan for how we wanted to start a family. Luckily, we had been living a lifestyle using only 50% of our earnings, which really saved us (as well as my redundancy payment). By the time restrictions were eased, I was already eight months pregnant, and we thought there was no point in me looking for a new job now as I would have to take maternity leave straight away. However, not being employed for over 10 months at this stage made me ineligible for any government parental payments, which was a surprise to me. So, no maternity leave, no government payments and one income with a new baby was something we had to navigate.

How did you navigate parental leave?

Once I was made redundant, Teresa started to look for full-time work. She easily found a role that covered our financial needs (two mortgages and living costs for three of us). But after I gave birth to Grayson in March 2021 and Teresa took three of her planned six weeks off, she moved roles, forfeiting the second half of her parental leave. This gave her a higher income, giving me the ability to stay home with the new baby.

How has having children changed your family's financial goals and lifestyle?

With Teresa working from home more and our baby quickly turning into a toddler, our apartment was getting cramped. We no longer had to be close to the city to work, and I wanted to be closer to family. So, we sold our apartment and bought a much bigger house 20 km from the city, close to family, for less than what we sold our apartment for.

Before having a kid I thought of not working as 'sacrificing' my career, but now I consider myself very lucky to have this time with her.

How are you thinking about generational wealth for your child?

Currently we have a savings account for Grayson, which we contribute $100 a month to and will put all her birthday and Christmas monetary gifts into. I also plan to tax Grayson's allowance and start the conversation around tax and what it goes towards.

Another idea I have is to discuss lifestyle with her – the type and location of dwelling she might want to live in, the car she might want to drive, holidays she might want to go on, kids she might want to have – and what costs are associated with those things. This will give her an idea of what she might need to earn to have this lifestyle, and this might help her choose a path that also aligns with her interests and natural abilities. This is something I wish my parents had done with me.

Your daughter has a viral TikTok video and is now making money through an agency. How are you teaching her about finances through this experience?

By pure luck, this video has given our family a few hundred dollars each month. I put all the money we earn from the video into Grayson's saving account. This will be a great learning opportunity for her regarding passive income and how it works.

Do you have any advice for new parents?

Here are some questions to discuss with your partner:

- Do you know exactly where your money is going?
- How much are you willing to invest in education?
- How many cars do you need, and what type? What are the running costs?
- Do you need a bigger house, or one that's closer to schools, family, work or support?
- What support system do you have?
- What's your mental and emotional health looking like?
- Do you plan to pay for child care? What costs are involved?
- What's your current level of understanding of money management? Do you need to learn more to help your child with their finances?
- What type of holidays do you want?
- Do you need to earn more or get a new job?
- What if you can't conceive naturally? Have you considered the costs of fertility assistance?

I believe if you're aware of these things, you'll be able to make better decisions and act faster.

What was the best piece of advice you've received regarding parenthood?

Be present. Be in the moment as much as you can. No amount of money can buy this time back. Once it's gone, it's gone.

Chapter 7

How to invest for your child and grow their wealth: Investing for kids

'There is no better investment of time and money than in the life of a child. They are the future.'

Alma Powell

A 2021 report by Finder found that 7% of children under 12 have an investing brokerage account. Parents are thinking of their children's future, ensuring their money compounds over the long term. Shares generally increase in value despite short-term fluctuations in the market, and many long-term investors agree with the saying, 'It's time in the market, not timing the market', emphasising long-term investing over picking 'winning shares'.

When my first child was born, I knew bub had the luxury of time when it came to investing. This is why I set up an account and started investing for my kid at the tender age of 6 months. In time, that small amount of cash will grow to be a large sum of money, even if another dollar isn't added. This is all due to the magic of compound interest, which I'll talk about shortly.

It's important to note that before investing for your kids, you should ensure that you've got your own finances covered and are in a good financial situation (as discussed in chapter 2). As they say on planes, you need to apply your own oxygen mask before assisting others. Similarly, making sure you are clear of any consumer debt, have an emergency fund and are projected to have enough money in retirement is of utmost importance before investing for your kids. Plus, it's best to invest money that you won't need access to for at least seven years. If you've got that sorted, then investing for your child may be a great option for you.

Knowing your 'why'

Having an idea of why you are investing is important to keep you focused on your long-term goal. Otherwise, it's easy to either get distracted, stop investing or try to tinker with your portfolio, all of which can sometimes be detrimental to the growth of your wealth.

My 'why' is that I want to have security for my family and ensure that my children have opportunities in the future. Plus, the thought of financial independence and work being optional (only working if I want to) is nice, too. Your 'why' may be different. Perhaps you want to have passive income or retire early. When it comes to your child, you may want to have a forced savings plan for their future or pay for their university. Or, maybe you just want to give them a head start in life.

Whatever your 'why', knowing it can keep you focused, which is important because long-term investing is a get-rich-slow strategy.

What is compound interest?

Often referred to as the eighth wonder of the world, compound interest is what makes investing so magical. Essentially, compound interest is when you earn interest on both the money you've saved and the interest you earn. Basically, your money makes money. That's what makes it magic.

Would you rather receive a million dollars right now or have a single cent double in value every day for 30 days? A million dollars sounds great, right? But if you wait just 30 days that cent would compound to over 5 million dollars! $5,368,709.12, to be exact. That's the power of compound interest.

You'd have 1 cent on the first day, 2 cents on the second day, on the third day you have 4 cents, and on the fourth day it compounds to 8 cents, which doesn't sound all that exciting. It gets really interesting when large amounts of money compound. So, on day 29 you would have $2,684,354, and the next day it would compound to $5,368,709; that's a difference of $2.684 million just by waiting an extra day (see table 7.1).

Table 7.1: demonstrating compound interest, doubling 1c over 30 days

Day 1	$.01	Day 16	$327.68
Day 2	$.02	Day 17	$655.36
Day 3	$.04	Day 18	$1,310.72
Day 4	$.08	Day 19	$2,621.44
Day 5	$.16	Day 20	$5,242.88
Day 6	$.32	Day 21	$10,485.76
Day 7	$.64	Day 22	$20,971.52
Day 8	$.1.28	Day 23	$41,943.04
Day 9	$2.56	Day 24	$83,886.08
Day 10	$5.12	Day 25	$167,772.16
Day 11	$10.24	Day 26	$355,544.32
Day 12	$20.48	Day 27	$671,088.64
Day 13	$40.96	Day 28	$1,342,177.28
Day 14	$81.92	Day 29	$2,684,354.56
Day 15	$163.84	Day 30	$5,368,709.12

Now, unfortunately, money doesn't usually double every day, or every year for that matter. Instead, the average return of the S&P 500, the main benchmark when it comes to investing, is 7%. Still, the example I've just given demonstrates in the simplest sense what exponential growth and compound interest does. It compounds using your existing savings and interest, and it continues to grow. The longer you wait the more it grows.

The famous investor Warren Buffett, who started investing at age 14, earned 99% of his net worth after his 50th birthday. He used time to his advantage to grow his money. The same goes for you and your children. The earlier you start investing for your kids, the longer the investing timeframe and the greater the potential for growing wealth.

Let's explore some more realistic examples now. If you saved $100 a week and hid that cash under your mattress for 40 years, you would have saved $208,000, which is a decent amount. It's definitely better than not saving at all. That said, if you saved that same $100 over 40 years in a bank account that paid you 2% in interest, your total savings would be $314,090, which is much better. However, if you invested $100 a week for 40 years into an investment that returned 7% a year, you would end up with $1,038,103. That's $830,103 more, just from investing rather than saving. As you can see in figure 7.1, your child could be a millionaire in 40 years by investing just $100 a week.

None of these examples include inflation which devalues your money over time (meaning you can buy less stuff now than you could five years ago). However, if inflation averages 3% to 4%, the first two options of hoarding money under your mattress or leaving it in a bank account would ultimately reduce your buying capacity – meaning you're actually losing dollars. Investing is a good option that lets you at least keep up with the rising costs of inflation.

Now back to that $100-a-week investment. For many families, $100 a week can be a large sum of money for those juggling parental leave, ECEC costs and adjusting to parenthood. Nonetheless, the concept of compound interest works for any amount of money, whether it's $5,

$500 or $5000. Compounding works exactly the same way. The earlier you start, the more time your money has to grow, and who doesn't want that for their family's future?

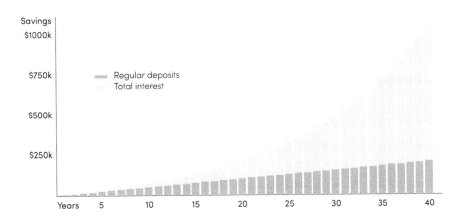

Figure 7.1: investing $100 a week for 40 years

Investing options for children

There are many reasons why you may want to invest for your child. Perhaps you want to have a forced savings plan for their future. Maybe you want to be able to help them out with a downpayment. Or possibly you just want to give them a head start in life. Creating generational wealth can truly change the financial trajectory of their life and be incredibly impactful.

Whatever the reason, there are various ways you can invest for your child. Each option comes with pros and cons, so it may be best to talk to a financial adviser to see which option is best suited to your family.

You can invest for your child via:

- your child's name
- an informal trust or minors' account
- a parent's name

- a family trust
- investment, insurance or education bonds
- superannuation.

Let's dive deeper into each of the investment options.

Investing in your child's name

There are many tax implications that you need to consider before choosing to invest directly in your child's name. (In fact, many brokerage platforms don't even provide the option to invest in a child's name but instead suggest that a parent invests as a trustee in the parent's name – see the next section for more on this). If your child is under 18 years of age and owns shares, they can only earn $416 tax-free per financial year (at the time of writing). That includes any dividend income. If they exceed this amount, you need to lodge a tax return on their behalf, and they may be taxed at the enormously high tax rate of 66%.

The reason the tax rate on unearned income for minors is so high is to discourage parents from avoiding tax by holding assets in their child's name. (Billionaires ruining things for ordinary families as per usual!) However, they may be exempt from this high tax rate under certain circumstances, such as:

- if the investments are funded by income from the child's work (such as a part-time job)
- if dividend income is from a deceased estate (such as a testamentary trust)
- if the child leaves school and commences full-time work
- if the child qualifies as disabled.

If those circumstances don't apply to your child, it may not be advantageous to hold assets directly in your child's name due to the extreme tax rate they would be charged. If the last circumstance applies, it may be worth looking into special disability trusts instead.

Investing through an informal trust or minors' account

Some parents want to avoid a formal trust and instead opt to create an account held 'in trust' for their child, who is a minor. This is also referred to as an 'informal trust', 'trustee account', 'minors account' or, in some cases, a 'custodial account'. This is different from a formal trust, which requires more complex accounting and paperwork.

The idea is simple: the parent acts as a custodian and can invest on behalf of the child, and once the child turns 18 the shares can be transferred into a new adult brokerage account held by the child. By law, the parent would be the legal owner of the shares and have full control of the investments, whereas the minor would be a beneficiary.

The parent would have to claim their tax file number (TFN) on the account and any income would be taxed to the parent. Otherwise, if they chose to use the child's TFN, then this would be similar to investing in the child's name (as per the previous section).

The advantage of this approach is that typically, capital gains tax (CGT) won't apply when there is no change to the beneficiary – in this case, the child for whom the investments were intended. This can be done via an off-market transfer, which is a private transaction that takes place outside of the share market. Often there is a fee associated with this off-market transaction via the brokerage platform.

Investing directly in your own name in a brokerage account

One of the simpler options is to invest for your child in your own name through your own brokerage account.

There are two main ways to do this. The first is that you can either open a new account with a new holder identification number (HIN) so you can separate the investments intended for your child from your own. This is kind of like opening a bank account, which requires some paperwork and verifying your identity. The benefit is that accounting is easier, since you can track capital gains and dividends because they are linked to the specific account.

The other option is to invest in your already established account. This option reduces the paperwork needed to open a new account, but it can get a little confusing if you are tracking the investments dedicated to them against your own. An option to create some clarity is to deliberately dedicate a specific asset to your child, such as an ETF, so that you can track the gains and dividends to make accounting easier.

Regardless of whether you choose to open a new account or use your existing one, this strategy is especially advantageous if the parent investing under their name has a low income and is subject to a low marginal tax rate. This is because any distribution of dividends will be taxed in the owner's name – so, if you are in a high-income bracket and you receive dividends on top of your income, you may enter into a higher tax bracket as your investments grow over time. The accounting during tax time is usually pretty straightforward in tracking dividend income, which you can access via your share registry (the organisation that manages the registry of shareholders).

The other thing to note is that because the investing parent is subject to the standard marginal tax rate, as opposed to the minor tax rate (the high rate applicable if you invest in a child's name), there can be a larger saving on the investments with this strategy.

Overall, this strategy isn't as tax-advantageous as investing through a trust or investment bonds, but it is quite flexible and easy to execute. For most families, this option is the most practical and tax-effective for their plans, given you can only maximise the benefits of most of the other options if you are already relatively comfortable financially.

The benefit of this strategy is that there are no restrictions on what you can invest in – whether that's shares, ETFs or bonds – or the time frame you can invest for. With this strategy, it's always easy to sell the assets whenever needed (which is referred to as 'liquidity'). It's also fairly low-cost as there's no initial set-up fee, especially if you choose a low-cost brokerage and index fund to invest in and have no complex tax obligations. Because this strategy is simple to set up and flexible in execution, it gives you total control over how the money is invested and what it can be used for.

When the time comes to transfer the ownership of the investments (or gift the shares) to your child, a CGT event may be triggered. There's no way to transfer investments to your child without it impacting the investing parent's taxable income, as CGT is applied to the account owner's marginal tax rate.

It may be advantageous to discuss with a financial adviser or tax accountant the best way to use this strategy, especially with regard to gifting your child investments while triggering CGT.

Investing via a family trust (or 'discretionary trust')

Investing through a family trust is a strategy often favoured by affluent families due to its substantial tax benefits. However, the initial setup costs (which can amount to a few thousand dollars) and ongoing accounting requirements may offset these benefits if the investment amount isn't substantial.

A family trust can be established with an individual, such as a parent, acting as the trustee. This individual has the authority to decide how the trust's assets are invested. They legally own the assets on behalf of the trust, while the family members, including the children, are the beneficiaries of the assets held in the trust.

The trustee, as the legal owner, is responsible for following the trust deed and deciding how to invest and distribute the money. For instance, in a family with a couple and two children, the trustee can distribute income from share dividends to any family member within the trust, considering their respective marginal tax rates. The trustee has the flexibility to distribute these assets to the children as they deem appropriate, either over several years or within a single year. Also, if structured correctly, a family trust can provide flexibility and asset protection because the trust can invest in various assets, such as shares and property, as it's considered a separate legal entity.

However, trusts don't allow you to overcome minor tax rates, so if you distribute taxable income above $416 in a financial year, hefty tax rates then apply, eroding the benefits of the tax structure. The offsetting benefit of buying investments through a family trust for a child is they can be transferred to them when their taxable income might result in no income tax being paid on the gain, or paid at the lowest marginal tax rate, after they turn 18. Also, while a family trust can offer tax advantages, it can be costly to establish and manage. There are restrictions on withdrawing an asset from the trust (the trust deed must allow it, and it must benefit the beneficiaries). It also requires additional accounting each tax year and a separate tax return for the trust. Therefore, this strategy is more beneficial when there's a substantial amount of money or assets within the trust. You also need to spend time upfront to get your trust deed right, as this says what you can and can't do, and it can be costly to change this later.

This strategy is typically recommended by financial advisers to higher-net-worth individuals or families with significant assets who can benefit from the tax advantages and asset protection offered by a family trust. However, for parents seeking a simpler, more affordable approach, other options might be more suitable. Consulting with a financial adviser and accountant when setting up a trust is recommended due to its complexity.

Investing via investment/insurance bonds

Don't be fooled by the name – investment bonds (also known as insurance bonds) aren't a traditional bond investment that you purchase on the stock exchange. An investment bond is an investment vehicle that provides tax benefits to those who want to invest for ten years or more and not tap into the money during this time. After ten years, you can withdraw your investment tax-free. While your investment is growing, any returns you earn before the ten years are up are taxed at 30% (and not included in your tax return, because they are taxed within the bond).

This is a great way to invest if your strategy is to 'set and forget'. You could use an investment bond to save for far-off purchases, such as your kids' university tuition, a car or assistance with their first house deposit.

As the investment bond is just the vehicle the investments are housed in, you still have the flexibility to decide what investments you purchase within the bond. Each investment bond provider generally has their own investment menu for you to choose from. Generally, you can pick from a range of index or actively managed funds.

There are some things to note within this option though. First, investment bonds have a 125% rule on contributions. This means, you can only contribute up to 125% of what you contributed the previous year. For example, if in the first year you contribute $10,000 the next year you can contribute up to $12,500. However, if you don't make a contribution one year, you will not be able to contribute in subsequent years. The reason being, 125% of $0 is $0. If you want to make an additional contribution, you will either need to start a new investment bond or restart your ten-year period. Some careful planning regarding continuous contributions may be worthwhile. Also, unless you're in a high-earning tax bracket, the tax advantage is negligible as investment bonds don't benefit from the 50% exemption on CGT for assets held more than 12 months. You'd have to crunch the numbers to see if it's worth it for your situation.

Unlike a super fund, there is flexibility in accessing the assets early if needed, but there may be tax implications based on when the funds are accessed. Picking the right investment bond can be quite complex, so it is worth talking with a financial adviser to work out which one is right for you. For example, there is a form of insurance bond known as an education bond, which provides further tax benefits if you are investing for your kid's education. Also, some providers are quite expensive, so it pays to do your research, because if you swap investment bond companies then your ten-year period resets.

An investment bond could be a good choice for a grandparent considering leaving a gift for their grandchild. They can arrange it so that the bond transfers to the child upon their passing as part of their estate planning, and they can even specify the age at which the child can access it tax free.

There's the ability to set up a child specific bond, but in most cases parents can act as the owner of the bond and transfer ownership to their child when they feel it's appropriate. Just make sure the bond provider allows transfers.

Investing through superannuation

This is probably a less known strategy, but it may be worth noting if you're considering all your options. Superannuation is one of the most tax-effective structures that exists in Australia with before-tax contributions being taxed at the rate of 15%, which is typically lower than an average person's marginal tax rate.

There are two main ways a parent can invest for their child via super. The first is to invest in their own account and eventually, when the parent meets a condition of release (the two most common being reaching age 60 and swapping employers, or reaching age 65), they can then access that money and gift it to their child, effectively using their own super as an investment vehicle for their child (as well as their retirement).

The other option, if your kid has started working and has a super account of their own, is to contribute to their super account. One of the biggest downsides to this strategy is that the child would need to meet a condition of release before they could access the money, which is typically retirement (at age 60 at the time of writing). Another condition of release is for a first home through the First Home Super Saver (FHSS) scheme if the child wants to purchase a primary residence. There are provisions that need to be met in order to release these funds for this scheme, and it may be a risky strategy if the child doesn't want to buy property, but it is an option nonetheless.

In theory, this strategy can set up your child for their own retirement, but if they want to access the money earlier they may be confined by legislative rules and changes, access restrictions and even restrictions on the ability to open a super fund for a minor. The investing timeline is very long, and since the investments are harder to access it may be less strategic if you want more flexibility for your child. Another disadvantage to consider is that the government has the ability to change rules around super (such as preservation age, tax rate and concessional contribution limit), all of which may affect this strategy. In fact, in 2023 new rules that are to be implemented in 2025 were introduced to tax earnings on super balances over $3 million, which could impact your child as compounding over time grows their nest egg.

Tax considerations when investing for your child

I know, I know, most people's eyes glaze over when they hear the words 'tax planning'. It's not my favourite topic either, but I've learned to embrace it, because you are doing a huge service for your kiddo and family by setting them up for success in the future. So, let's talk about taxes.

As you can probably guess, when investing for your child (or children), there are tax implications regardless of which option you choose. Which investment option you pursue comes down to personal preference and circumstance, but there are some things worth considering up front, such as who will be taxed (the adult, the trustee or the minor), how long are you planning to invest for and whether you're a low- or high-income earner.

If you choose to invest in your name or act as the trustee, all earnings, including dividends and capital gains, may be attributed to you. Because of this, some parents choose to invest in the lower-income-earner's name to reduce their taxes. This may be something you need to consider in your tax planning, as it can affect things like the income threshold for PLP and CCS (since these are based on your family income).

If your child is under 18 years of age and you choose to invest in their name, you may need to lodge a tax return for your child, especially if they earn more than $416 through investments (at the time of writing). As mentioned, the ATO taxes children's income earned through investments at an especially high rate of 66%, which includes any dividend income earned from the shares. The ATO website provides a comprehensive breakdown and examples of this, which is worth reading.

The main thing to remember when investing is that in most cases, taxes will need to be paid at some point due to dividends (income tax) and when the investment funds are transferred (CGT).

Investing in your child's future is great, of course, but it can be complicated. Hence, it's best to talk to an accountant or a financial adviser to understand which option is best for you.

Actionable steps

- Consider the various investing options for your child and seek advice from a financial adviser to ensure what's best for you and your family.
- Talk to a tax accountant about any concerns you have regarding investing for your child.
- If you are ready to start investing for your child, start now! There's no time like the present.

Katie

41 | husband (52), four children (14, 13, 10 and 7),
two cats | Qld

What was your upbringing around money?

I don't recall ever being taught a lot about money. I had one parent who worked away a lot – FIFO (fly-in fly-out) but not mining – with the intention of getting ahead and a stay-at-home parent who appeared to spend beyond their means. Some of this really only became apparent to me as I got older.

How did you prepare financially for parenthood?

Before we even got engaged we bought a house in a lower-cost area knowing our intention was to get married and start a family within five years. We committed to a mortgage that we could cover on one income knowing our priority was to have a stay-at-home parent for as long as possible.

As the main breadwinner, I banked leave and purchased leave to give myself as much time off as possible after each baby was born and before my husband took over as the stay-at-home parent for an extended time period.

Getting down to the nitty gritty, we also bought a lot of the big purchases second-hand with a focus on quality that would last through multiple kids. We were open to second-hand clothes and throughout the lives of our four kids had a whole lot of circular fashion happening through family and friends with young families.

How has having children changed your family's financial goals and lifestyle?

It really hasn't. In saying that, I'm very much a realist, so I'd say our goals aren't particularly lofty.

How are you thinking about generational wealth for your child?

This is a tough one. We weren't set up with anything by our families and potentially our kids won't get much of a head start going into adulthood either. This might seem like a cop out, but our focus is very much on funding extracurricular opportunities for our kids with the idea that they will hopefully open their eyes to broader possibilities as they get older.

How are you teaching your children about money and finances?

Perhaps passively. Budgeting is a very open conversation in our house. Each of our kids has their own bank account, which we deposit into fortnightly (very small amounts) to build a small nest egg for when they are maybe ready to buy a car (or similar). We don't do pocket money but we have broader conversations and provide opportunities for them to save for bigger items. Things like tax and superannuation or retirement planning are also a very regular topic given our jobs – my husband and I are both public servants in fields related to those topics.

Is there anything you wish you knew prior to having kids?

No, we planned well and long term to be in the position we are. It's played out as anticipated (noting that our plan had a fair degree of room to be flexible and pivot as needed.

Actually, maybe the one thing I wish I'd known is that I'd get severe post-natal depression after three of four babies. Even with private health insurance that still added big costs for us – not insurmountable and not particularly future-changing, but certainly not something we factored in.

Do you have any advice for new parents?

Plan ahead as far in advance as you possibly can. Aim to have flexibility in your budget (and your calendar!) for unexpected events. And don't prioritise 'new' (house, car or products).

What was the best piece of advice you've received regarding parenthood?

The days are long but the years are short. Good, bad or otherwise, every phase is exactly that – a phase. Oh, and 'little kids, little problems; big kids, big problems' – invest the time to know and grow your littlies so that when they get bigger, they come to you with the bigger, scarier stuff.

Sandra

43 | partner (47), one child (13) | Brisbane, Qld

What was your upbringing around money?

Both parents worked full-time from when I was three, but one was a teacher and so was home for school holidays. This was before long daycare, but we did family daycare locally and one of our grandparents came to stay sometimes. My parents owned their home and saved up to renovate. They had savings accounts for us kids that we used to get our first (old, second-hand) cars. My parents were very keen on us doing further study and choosing professions that allowed options – work for government, private or yourself; full-time or part-time; in Queensland, around Australia or overseas. We did have to pay all of our own HECS, car and transport expenses, mobile phones and so on, but they were happy to house and feed us while we were studying.

How did you prepare financially for parenthood?

We bought our house two years prior to having a baby. We borrowed below what the bank would give us as we had just moved back to Australia, my partner was contracting and I worked variable hours, neither of us permanent. We bought in a location with good public transport and airport links, close to schools, shops and so on, so we only needed one car. We deliberately chose Brisbane due to lower cost of living and being closer to family. We pushed hard to get the mortgage down early so we had breathing space for parental leave.

Do you and your partner have a similar money mindset?

I'm a researcher and saver; they'll spend when they need or want something. I know our overall position and when we have spare cash or need to rein it in. We discuss larger purchases or get quotes and plan as needed. We tend to be 'value' people, willing to save up and pay more for things like clothes, shoes, luggage, appliances, furniture and cars that will last us longer or are more energy- or cost-efficient over time. We also make sure we give some away as we realise we are very fortunate.

How has having children changed your family's financial goals and lifestyle?

Less travel, but we still aim to do that – both Australia and overseas to see family. We go out for breakfast rather than dinner, and less often. My partner used to travel a lot more but now tries to work close to home or from home, and I work local and permanent part-time to manage childcare, after-school activities and being home for dinner.

How are you thinking about generational wealth for your child?

We started a high-interest savings account for baby after birth and consistently saved a little in there each payday. Once it reached a few thousand, we started investing in ETFs. Knowing what I know now, I'd have invested the money earlier.

How are you teaching your children about money and finances?

We talk about what's on special and when things go up or down in price. We talk about petrol prices, and how big the tank is in the car and how far you can drive with that much petrol. We talk about how many hours it might take to 'earn' something. We did pocket money and money jars. My child has a 'budget' for tuck shop at school for the term (equivalent to about one lunch per week, so they need to watch the balance). We have a family spreadsheet with what's in our various accounts and what our bills are, and my child has own section in there with their accounts so they can see their 'net worth'.

Is there anything you wish you knew prior to having kids?

School hours and work hours don't match. Also, flexibility is needed the whole journey: we've done grandparents, long daycare, government-subsidised kindy with after-hours care, au pairs, uni-student babysitters, swapping with other parents, working from home, using long-service leave, adjusting work hours, vacation care… and we only have one child!

Do you have any advice for new parents?

Smaller birthday parties are easier. Buy, sell and swap clothes, toys, and school uniforms as they need them or grow out of them. The local library and playgroup can be awesome resources.

What was the best piece of advice you've received regarding parenthood?

Never wear shoes you can't run in!

Chapter 8

How to set up your kid for financial success

'We need a financial revolution in this country, and it needs to start with our kids.'

Scott Pape

Babies are born with the basic concept of numeracy. In a study of infant brains, researchers found that babies were able to detect mathematical errors – their brains showed similar patterns to those of adults when looking at incorrect equations. This means that, fundamentally, mathematics is an innate part of our human existence. (I'm sure we can all agree that maths is more intuitive than spelling.) Now, I know not everyone identifies with maths and numbers, and some of us may still be carrying the limiting belief that we aren't good at maths; however, if we voice these beliefs, our children notice. The influence of parents, teachers and friends has a profound effect on how they engage with maths and, in turn, financial literacy.

So, let's discuss financial literacy among our kids. Unfortunately, financial literacy among Australian youth is in decline, dropping almost half a year of schooling from 2012 to 2018 in a report conducted by the Australian Council for Educational Research (ACER). In fact, according to the Household, Income and Labour Dynamics in Australia (HILDA) Survey, students were not able to answer five basic financial questions, scoring 2.9 out of 5 in 2020, down from the 2016 score of 3.4. This begs the question: who should be teaching financial literacy to our kids? Some believe it's the job of the schools, while others defer to the financial institutions and banks. Unfortunately, if parents don't take on this role, there's a large likelihood that our kids will miss out on critical financial education.

Australian students have a bigger spread between the highest and lowest financial literacy scores than any other country, according to the ACER study. However, there are a few factors that contribute to this massive gap. Students from lower socioeconomic backgrounds were overwhelmingly outperformed by those from higher socioeconomic backgrounds, as were First Nations youth by non–First Nations youth. Furthermore, financial literacy is especially poor in kids living in rural areas and from immigrant families whose main language isn't English. It's apparent that there is a lot of economic disparity when it comes to access to financial education, but it appears that there is still a lot of room for improvement when it comes to educating our kids on finances.

It's one thing to just test our kids' understanding of financial literacy; it's another to understand the system in which they are learning. Although we discussed in depth in chapter 1 how we as parents can adjust our own money mindsets to support our kids as they navigate the world financially, there's still a lot that can be done within our schools to support teachers in educating our kids, especially given 90% of parents think personal finance should be taught in schools.

While 75% of teachers claim to be financially literate, only half feel confident enough to actually teach finances. Furthermore, 38% of maths teachers teaching Years 7 to 10 aren't even qualified in mathematics. Now, I know teachers are doing their best, and this isn't to lay the blame on them; it's just a systemic issue that kids aren't getting the practical financial skills they need to take on the real world.

The truth is that students do want to learn about finances, with 62% of them being interested in learning about investing. But with students opting to drop maths due to its lack of relevance to everyday life, and enrolment into Year 12 economics classes declining, there isn't a lot of opportunity to learn about financial concepts that relate to them directly.

Research shows that there are two forms of education that significantly improve financial outcomes: maths and personal finance education. It makes sense, right? Maths is just numbers and equations without context, whereas personal finance includes the context of psychology and behaviour. The two complement one another to deliver financial literacy. However, if students feel as though maths has little relevance, they most likely harbour a negative feeling towards the subject, making it very hard to change this belief, which can continue into adulthood.

Combine the systemic barriers of the education system with corporations and banks competing for the attention of our kids – with 40% of people staying loyal to their banks into adulthood, you can see why it's a huge business – and it's a massive challenge to guide our children towards positive financial outcomes and set them up for financial success.

We need to remember that we, the parents, are the biggest influence on our kids when it comes to money, so we need to take it upon ourselves to teach, support and guide them. If we don't teach them, it may be that no one else will.

The fundamentals of teaching personal finance to kids

Whether your kid is three or 13, it's never too early to start teaching your child numeracy and the value of money. By age three, children have an understanding of numbers. At age five, they understand basic monetary concepts around coins, change and buying items. By age seven, children can already grasp concepts around budgeting and delayed gratification when it comes to savings. Most of these concepts can easily be taught by parents. And since parents are their main source of financial education and literacy, it's paramount that you empower your kids by teaching them the fundamentals of personal finance.

Before we dive into the fundamentals, here are some tips for talking about finances with your kids:

- Start talking about money concepts when they are young – they are sponges and understand more than you think.
- Speak openly and try to avoid negative language when discussing money.
- Use relatable examples and age-appropriate topics so that your kids can connect with them easily.
- Use visuals to illustrate ideas or help with reaching goals (such as a savings tracker).
- Don't forget to make it fun!

So, let's dive into the fundamentals of teaching personal finance:

- teaching the value of money
- normalising money conversations
- using real-life examples
- instilling good money habits.

Teaching the value of money

For many kids, their introduction to money is through the concept of acquiring things. Parents work, they make money; money buys toys and food. Money is a means to acquire objects and things. But it's only when children get older that they really understand the value of money and its connection to time (but we will get to that later).

When kids are younger, the idea that money provides us with the ability to purchase things allows children to understand the necessity of money. Without it, we can't eat, or have a home, or take holidays together. Hence, money is very important to our family. But to understand how money works and how it can be used, kids need access to some of their own money as well.

Allowances and pocket money

One of the easiest ways for kids to grasp the value of cash is through allowances or pocket money. Providing an allowance can be a controversial topic, but regardless of whether you're for or against, it's important to consider that an exchange (such as chores for money) is more impactful than just giving money without any expectation. The exchange of money for something is a valuable lesson as it provides a sense of accomplishment, solidifies the idea that money can be traded for a service and is a simulation of real-life reciprocity. This also empowers the child to make their own choices, such as whether they want to do the chore for money, how they will spend the money and how much of it they will save.

The benefit of receiving an allowance is twofold. First, it provides a visual aid: seeing money add up over time – whether you use money jars, savings accounts or an allowance app – is powerful. Second, it provides the ability to allocate money to various goals, such as spending (on everyday items), saving (for a larger purchase, such as a toy or a car), giving (to a charity or to help someone) and, in some cases, investing (usually reserved for older kids once they understand the other three options). Dividing cash between these options means that some prioritisation and compromise needs to happen, especially if it is enforced that every time they receive money, each jar gets some (see figure 8.2 overleaf).

An allowance is a great stepping stone to the real world of earning money. It provides confidence, opportunity and the ability to understand how money can be used. With the rise in digital payments, kids see cash less frequently, making it harder for them to understand how money works. Providing them with the opportunity to use real money, while also giving them the chance to understand how to make cashless purchases, can aid them in grasping these concepts more easily. By managing their own money, kids are able to

Figure 8.1: a suggested timeline of children's financial actions and lessons

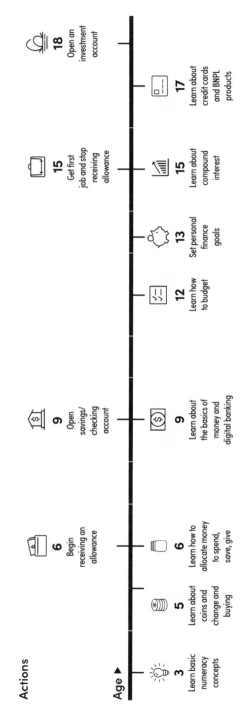

Actions

6 Begin receiving an allowance

9 Open savings/checking account

15 Get first job and stop receiving allowance

18 Open an investment account

Age ▶

3 Learn basic numeracy concepts

Lessons

5 Learn about coins and change and buying

6 Learn how to allocate money to spend, save, give

9 Learn about the basics of money and digital banking

12 Learn how to budget

13 Set personal finance goals

15 Learn about compound interest

17 Learn about credit cards and BNPL products

SOURCE: ADAPTED FROM MERRILL

learn how to spend wisely, practice delayed gratification while saving, practice generosity through philanthropy and experience the power of compounding when investing (but we will talk about that later).

On top of that, it enables your child to set goals for each option and choose how to navigate and balance their wants and needs. Of course, we all cringe when we see our kids spending money on Pokémon, but that's all part of the learning experience. It's as important to learn about spending money as saving money, which is why pocket money is the cornerstone of understanding how money works.

Figure 8.2: allocating pocket money

Time, delayed gratification and quality versus quantity

The saying 'time is money' was coined by Benjamin Franklin and illustrates the idea that time is a valuable resource. Most of us exchange our time for money (unless we have some source of passive income), hence we are bound to the clock. Our time is finite, and although we would rather be doing other things, including spending time with our kids, we still need to pay the bills.

This concept is also true for children. If they don't do their chore for the week or go to their after-school job, they won't get paid. Providing them with the opportunity to see that there is a trade-off between time and money is valuable in building their understanding of how the world works.

There are also some valuable conversations you can have with your child around the value of time and money, such as around:

- delayed gratification (for example, taking longer to save for a bike versus spending money on stickers, which are quicker to acquire)
- the value of money and how to use it (through questions like, 'If you had $1000, what would you do with it?)
- wage and time (for example, 'If your salary was $10 an hour versus $100 an hour for a 40-hour work week, how long would it take to earn $10,000, or $100,000?')
- how many hours need to be worked to purchase an item (for example, how many weeks would it take to save allowance money for a doll house? Or how many hours would they have to work their part-time job to buy a video game? Is that item worth that many hours of work?)
- the convenience versus the cost of items (for example, taking public transit over walking).

Each of these examples weighs up the value of time and money. Like money, time needs to be budgeted for. In fact, time is more valuable than money because it's finite – you can always make more money, but you can't make more time. It's valuable to talk to your child about how they spend their free time. Exploring what they value, such as spending time with family or exploring new interests or hobbies, allows them to consider how they can acquire more time to do these things.

Ultimately the only way to 'buy' time is by having more money so that you don't have to spend time working. The best way to do this is through investing. Think of it this way: you go to work to make money, but if you use that money to make more money then you won't need to spend as much time working, because your money is working for you. This is called a 'passive income', and this concept can be taught through the power of compound interest (as discussed in chapter 7).

To expand on that, the value of money is higher now than it would be at a future date due to its earning potential – if you invest money now, it can grow, but if you invest it later then it has less time to grow. Again, this concept can be illustrated through compound interest, showing how impactful it is to start investing as early as possible. Now, these concepts are a tad complex and should be reserved for older kids, but they are interlinked with the idea of delayed gratification, which can be taught to younger kids.

The famous marshmallow experiment studied children's ability to delay gratification. Kids were offered a marshmallow and told that if they didn't eat their marshmallow in the allotted time, they would receive a second one. Kids who showed more restraint and had the ability to delay gratification performed better over time in academics and social skills, and had better outcomes overall. Learning to resist the temptation of immediate pleasure with the goal of receiving a more valuable reward later on is another life skill that will enable our children to withstand challenges in life, monetary or otherwise.

For the longest time I used a second-hand vacuum that barely sucked up dust from my carpet. I refused to buy a new one because I didn't want to spend the money, but every week, when it was time to clean the house, I dreaded lugging out the heavy, poorly sucking vacuum. It was so cumbersome, since it required me to plug it in and unplug it in every room, but I somehow believed I was winning out due to saving money by not buying a new appliance. Then one day, when I was complaining about our horrible vacuum, my partner suggested we just buy a new one for Christmas. Lo and behold, my cordless Dyson is a godsend. In fact, I question why I chose to struggle with a poorly working machine for so long, making me dread the household chore and wasting so much time and effort. The point of my long-winded story is that saving money isn't always the best course of action, and sometimes it's necessary to weigh up the pros and cons of quality as well.

The value of quality is an important lesson for kids to learn. The fake LEGO set may be cheaper but do the pieces fit together as well as the real LEGO? Is it better to hold out and save for the better set of headphones or buy the cheaper, flimsier pair? When it comes to money, quality and how much time it takes to save, there's always a trade-off.

When it comes to quality, second-hand items may be a better option than buying new, especially when it comes to the savings. Would your child prefer to have five second-hand toys or buy one brand-new item with their hard-earned money? Ultimately, if an item is bought brand-new, as soon as it comes out of the packaging it's already second-hand. These are the types of lessons that kids learn through trial and error. As much as it can be painful seeing them make mistakes, that is the best way for them to learn.

As we say in the tech industry, 'fail fast, fail often', which highlights the importance of failure as a natural part of learning. By allowing our children to make their own choices and mistakes along the way, we enable them to learn quickly. As they learn, we can actively support them in growing and evolving a better money mindset.

In order to guide and support our kids, we need to ensure that we can have open, transparent and non-judgemental conversations with them about money. So let's talk about that next.

Normalising money conversations

Research shows that people are more likely to talk about sex and politics than money. In Australia, about half the population would rather avoid the topic altogether. Luckily, millennials are more willing to discuss money than their parents, and hopefully, if that trend continues, so will our children. By removing the taboo around money conversations, we can create open discourse around finances, allowing curious minds to ask questions and learn through our guidance.

Money conversations can lead to better financial decisions that can have a lifelong impact. The only people that benefit from not talking about money are those in power – whether it be the company that may be underpaying you or the bank that is profiting off your lack of understanding around credit cards. Money conversations tend to demystify and provide transparency, which ultimately benefits you and your kids (see figure 8.3).

Figure 8.3: great conversations lead to great decisions

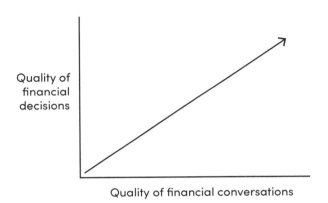

Quality of financial decisions

Quality of financial conversations

I grew up being told to never talk about how much I earn. In my first job after university, I was chatting with a colleague who was my age (we were the youngest employees at the company) and she revealed her salary – and, to my shock, I realised that I was being significantly underpaid. Learning the truth was hard, but it inspired me to negotiate a raise and prepared me for my next job. If my parents had had more open conversations about income and negotiating for a job, I could have started that position at a higher wage. But alas, it was something I learned the hard way. The belief I held – that it was rude to talk about how much I made – was a direct result of my family's money culture.

Family money culture and dinner-table chats

Each family has their own inside jokes, vibe and culture. Mine include a lot of silly songs about one another and playful teasing. Yours might include a lot of wordplay and cuddles on the couch. Whatever your family culture is, consider how money plays into it.

From a young age, having open and honest conversations helps children navigate their understanding of the world. Counting and playing with coins is a great first step for little ones. Discussing why Mummy has to go to work or why Daddy is trying to find the best deal on coffee beans should be a regular household occurrence (because coffee is life, and no one wants to overpay for coffee). Actively talking about how money affects our lives allows our children to notice all of the different intersections of finance.

If culture is the ideas, customs and social behaviour of a group of people, then money culture encompasses the ideas, customs and behaviours around finance. Just as different countries have different cultures when it comes to finance – China statistically has a higher savings rate relative to other countries, in Germany cash is the preferred payment of choice and in India physical gold is a favoured asset – our families have their own micro money cultures.

Thinking about your family's money culture can allow you to recognise what money beliefs your children are absorbing. Whether it's intense frugality or frivolous spending, you are upholding the cultural dynamics around finances. Similarly, your reactions reinforce your family's money culture. Are you blasé about a missed credit card payment or furious, or somewhere in between? Your family money culture plays into your children's beliefs and will impact them as they grow into adulthood.

It's easy to get emotional about money. Studies show we are more likely to be upset by money we lose than happy about money we gain. However, it may be advantageous to approach money and finance in a neutral manner. Some things can be disappointing (such as interest-rate hikes) and others can be exciting (like getting shoes on sale), but ensuring that money is portrayed as neither good nor evil but instead as a means to life can reinforce a more positive relationship with finances.

By normalising these conversations, it's easier to understand what your child values. Whether that's pride in saving coins in their money box or empathy and gratitude when they donate to the local homeless shelter, learning about your child's own money mindset is valuable in supporting them in their own goals.

Of course, money conversations evolve as children grow. In the early days, conversations may only be about what money can buy. As they get older, conversations may revolve around the economics of the household and, as they become teenagers, the reality of managing their own job, taxes and super. The point is that it's never too early to start talking about money.

One of the best times to have money conversations is over family dinner. There are many benefits to sharing a meal together, including increased confidence and communication, which can aid organic money chats. Ensure you share your own money wins and losses and how you think about them. This provides practical advice and a blueprint for how they themselves can navigate the pros and cons of their own money choices. By normalising these discussions in everyday settings, the topic of money becomes less taboo and equips kids with financial literacy and confidence.

Using real-life examples

Many kids don't connect with maths in school because it doesn't seem relevant to the real world, and there's so much fixation on formulas with very little focus on the underlying concepts. Long division, polynomials and calculus can all move over and make way for concepts that make more sense, like using maths to calculate net worth or percentages that are allocated to budgets. Using maths concepts in real-life settings can, along with financial literacy, set up your child for success in the future.

One of the easiest real-life examples is the experience of pocket money, which we already discussed. Other ways kid can learn about money are through examples that come up at home, in running their own business, when they start a job, and through philanthropy. Each experience will be useful for them; just ensure to keep it fun, use visuals and engage with them at their own level.

Home economics

There are so many real-life examples at home that kids can learn from. When they're little, it's fun to pretend with examples as well. With my toddler, we often play a game where we pretend to go to work (where we earn coins) and then we go shopping (to give away our coins). It's a simple game, but because so many transactions are digital, this is already setting up my child with a basic understanding of exchanging time for money. As kids get older, practical tasks can teach them invaluable lessons – and save or earn your household some money in the process.

Here are some ideas that can encourage kids to take an interest in the household economics:

- When grocery shopping, discuss the difference between value and price.
- Encourage your child to throw a party within a budget and manage costs.
- Provide your kid with lunch money for the month and get them to budget their cash.
- Give them some money back if they purchase an item that is useful for the house while discussing the concept of taxes.
- When shopping for a new item, get them to search and compare pricing to find the best discount.
- If they are asking for a pet, get them to draft up a budget that gives a realistic idea of how much it will cost and how much time it will take to look after.
- Similarly, if they want to buy a car, get them to draft up a budget of how much it will cost, including petrol, maintenance and insurance.

- Get them to take note of all the different scams the house has been targeted by (via email, phone, etc.) and explain what to avoid.
- Pull out your electricity or gas bill and see if your kid can shop around and find you a better deal.
- Encourage them to sell some household items that are no longer used.
- Get them to calculate all the subscriptions the household has and identify if any of them could be cancelled or swapped for a cheaper option.
- Challenge them to save the household money on internet and mobile bills by shopping around.

Each of these suggestions can be modified or even monetised – for example, if the kid saves or makes money, then maybe that amount could go into their bank account. The goal is to have open discourse and help them learn practical skills that will empower them in the future.

Building a business

One of the best ways to learn is with hands-on experience (also known as kinaesthetics), whereby kids can engage with something in the real world to solidify concepts in their head. When it comes to economics, there's really no better way to learn than to start your own business. Whether it's a lemonade stand, selling bespoke candles or becoming a social media influencer, the business lessons are the same: revenue minus expenses equals profit. However, the challenges that come with running a business can differ depending on the venture. That's why this is one of the most rewarding yet challenging projects your child can take on.

Starting and running a business taps into many skills that can be transferable to a first job. It requires an eclectic skill set – from customer acquisition, to marketing, to understanding if the product or service is really something that people want and need. But the best part of starting a business is feeling valuable and knowing someone is willing to pay you for your effort.

As a parent, supporting any entrepreneurial skills your child possesses or shows interest in will pay dividends. The critical thinking it takes to consider all aspects of a business makes it an exciting project to work on; plus, they can add it to their résumé. These lessons will empower and create confident kids that will grow into resilient employees – or, better yet, employers – one day.

Supporting them to earn their own money

In many ways, a first job is a rite of passage as a teenager. It provides responsibility, autonomy and, of course, cash to spend on whatever is desired. However, money skills aren't just acquired, they are learned, so if your child doesn't know how to manage $100 then they won't know how to manage $100,000.

As parents, it's important for us to be there supporting our kids as they navigate pay cheques, how much to save and spend, taxes and, of course, their super. Set up a bank account with them and discuss ahead of time how much they are planning to put aside, potentially replicating the buckets of spend, save, give and invest. Remind them that as they take on new roles, they should ensure their super is consolidated in order to save on fees. Plus, take the time to explain how the taxes on their earnings help to build schools, roads and hospitals to better their understanding of their impact in the community.

Yes, it's their money, but while they are still under your roof navigating the corporate world it's important that you are giving them your full support and helping them make the best financial decisions for themselves.

Philanthropy, volunteering and donations

Studies show that doing an act of kindness makes us happier and improves our mental health. What better way to show kindness to someone than through philanthropy, volunteering or giving donations?

As much as money is empowering in many ways, it's also one of the biggest sources of inequality in the world. Privilege plays a huge part in a person's successes, yet it's something that may not seem obvious at first glance.

By bringing awareness to poverty and the unequal distribution of wealth, children are able to broach difficult topics while feeling as though they are making a small impact. This can build empathy, understanding and gratitude, and a life-long habit of giving to others.

Instilling good money habits

Being good with money has less to do with maths and more to do with behaviour. Fortunately, behaviour and habits can be taught (as per chapter 1). But like any skill, it has to be taught repetitively to become part of a child's routine. Whether it's brushing teeth after breakfast, making the bed as soon as they wake or depositing 10% of their pay into a savings account, automated routines and systems feel effortless as they require little managing and thinking.

The behavioural side of personal finance is the most challenging. Mentally, we may know it's better to leave our money in our investments, but emotionally we may want to pull them out when the market is in a downturn. Similarly, kids may know it makes sense to put their money into savings, but emotionally they may want to spend it on a new game. By teaching and supporting our children to build strong money habits, we can empower them to weather any financial storm that blows their way.

Studies suggest that kids are most influenced by parents during childhood and adolescence (around age 12), and as children navigate their teen years they are more susceptible to the social influence of their peers and other adults. Once they get to adulthood, their susceptibility to influence is reduced. I'm sure we can all remember our teenage years and how uncool our parents seemed. Now couple that with trying to teach personal finance and the cool factor plummets even further. Therefore, timing financial lessons while kids are young and impressionable (and open to their parents' influence) can ensure optimal influence and acceptance of money concepts.

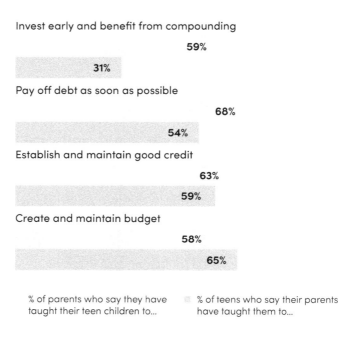

Figure 8.4: financial lessons given and received

Invest early and benefit from compounding

59%

31%

Pay off debt as soon as possible

68%

54%

Establish and maintain good credit

63%

59%

Create and maintain budget

58%

65%

% of parents who say they have taught their teen children to...

% of teens who say their parents have taught them to...

SOURCE: MERRILL

So, what are some of the most important money habits? Let's dive in.

Pay yourself first

One of my favourite sayings in personal finance is 'pay yourself first'. Essentially, this means that you put aside a percentage of every pay cheque for yourself. As a kid, I remember putting $1 of every $10 I earned away in my piggy bank (which was actually shaped like a turtle – random, I know!); over time that money grew, and I didn't even notice the impact of the 10% of my pay that I stashed away.

I wish I'd had the knowledge at the time to take that 10% and invest it, instead of allowing it to lose value in my turtle bank due to inflation. But hindsight is 20/20, and since I can't go back in time, at least I can let my kids learn from my mistake.

(I've continued to pay myself first to this day. The only adjustment I've made is that I've increased the percentage I save and invest. I guess some habits die hard. This is definitely a lesson I learned from my parents.)

Stay out of debt

Some of life's big lessons begin with opening a bank account. Some banks charge fees, which is why it's important to find one that offers a fee-free, high-interest savings account. Financial institutions are very lucrative and loyalty doesn't usually benefit customers. Therefore, shopping around for better interest rates is a practical habit for our kids to take on as they start to save larger amounts of money.

Credit card offers are a smart way to lure customers into debt. (I mean, how else will they make money?) Discussing some of the different ways you can pay for purchases provides an opportunity to discuss different products, such as cash, credit, loans and Buy Now Pay Later (BNPL) products. Because we are living in a digital age, it can be a struggle to connect with money leaving a bank account and not overspend, especially if you have easy access to debt. It's a good reminder to think of debt as 'not your money' but the bank's, and in order to access it, it will need to be paid off at a higher cost.

It's also worth noting that not all debt is equal. Some debts, like mortgages, are considered appreciating assets, meaning they usually go up in value over time. On the other hand, high-interest debts (such as credit card debt, personal loans or consumer debt) are depreciating assets, meaning they go down in value over time. An Xbox isn't going to go up in value, but a house may help increase your wealth over time and also provides a place to live.

It's essential to teach your kids about credit card debt, BNPL schemes, student loans, personal loans and mortgages and how each of these debts can affect their financial goals.

Debt compounds in the same way that investments compound. With credit card interest rates averaging 19.94% and personal loans 10.02%, this can really set a person back (see figure 8.5).

Figure 8.5: debt can set you back

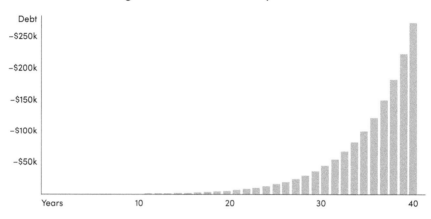

If your child took on a $100 debt and didn't pay it back, after ten years the interest on that debt would be $623. The longer it takes to pay off the debt, the larger it grows. So, after 20 years it would be $5121, in 30 years $37,623 and in 40 years $272,464 at 19.94% interest. That's all on just a $100 debt.

At time of writing, Australians have accrued a whopping $17.73 billion in credit card debt. Surely, your kid won't be one of them. Or you can say what my parents said to me: 'Never get a credit card unless you are 100% sure you can pay it off every month, and if you're not sure, use cash'.

Grow your wealth

Does your kid want to be a millionaire? Well, it's possible! By investing an initial $1000 at age 20 and then investing $400 monthly, with an assumed return of 7% interest your child can retire with $1,066,237 (see figure 8.6).

Figure 8.6: how to become a millionaire

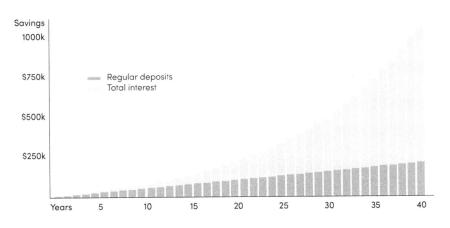

SOURCE: MONEYSMART

Now, the idea of being a millionaire may sound really cool, but it can also be somewhat abstract. (Does a kid really understand what a million dollars can buy them?) Plus, anything long-term feels like a lifetime to a kid!

That's why talking about how investing works (which we covered in chapter 6) can be really impactful. Plus, if they've started a job, they are already investing through their super. Walk them through the different investment options their super has, talk to them about the fee structure, and ensure they only have one super and consolidate if they're signed up to a few funds (which can happen as part of onboarding to a new job).

But what makes investing relatable to kids is explaining that they can actually own a part of a company. Now, how many kids can say that?

They may shop at Coles and Woolworths, and use an iPhone. They may watch Disney and Netflix, and eat at McDonald's. All of these companies are listed, meaning they can own a share in them. Framing investing as owning a piece of a company, which makes profits and often grows in value, can really spark interest in growing their wealth.

Using the concept of 'pay yourself first' by investing a percentage of each pay cheque can have a profound impact on their future wealth. Whether they invest into their super or outside of super depends on their specific circumstances, so it may be best to talk to a financial adviser. Nonetheless, small habits make a big difference. In fact, chances are they won't even notice that they are putting a small amount of money aside to grow and compound. That's the beauty of having time on your side.

With compound interest, time is your best friend. The earlier a kid starts to invest, the longer they have for their money to grow – as long as they promise to not pull it out early, as they will lose out on the opportunity cost of building wealth and hopefully becoming a millionaire.

Just a reminder: investing comes with risk, and past performances are not an indicator of future returns, so it's important that you walk your child through the risks associated with investing. The stock market can be volatile, and fluctuations in the market are a very normal part of the process.

Automating your finances

The funny thing about investing is that the more you adjust your portfolio, the higher the likelihood of it underperforming. It's totally counterintuitive! With most things in life you need to work hard to get better results, but with finances, the less you tinker with them, the better off you'll usually be (provided they're set up right to begin with).

Automating your finances removes the need for constantly monitoring your money or making emotional decisions. Plus, it frees up your time, and what kid doesn't want to have more time on their hands?

As your kid starts to manage their own money, automating some of their expenses or savings will help them build smart habits as their financial landscape widens.

Things that may be worth automating for your child include:

- 'paying yourself first', whether that be into a savings account or an investment account (or both!)
- paying off their credit card (if they have one) – by paying off your card monthly, you are avoiding any interest on the debt
- paying their phone bill, because doing this on time is a good starting point for kids as they start to take on more expenses.

Although automating their finances is a step in the right direction, there are some automated expenses that can have a negative impact on their finances. I'm talking about subscriptions. Spotify, Netflix and Audible all rely on a subscription model, locking you into a regular paying cadence. It's fine to pay for these services if you use them regularly, but if you forget about them and they continue to charge you, they can eat into your budget quickly, especially if you aren't using them. Setting a reminder in the calendar to regularly check their bank account is a good way for your children to stay on top of automated expenses and ensure financial wellness.

Live within your means

Morgan Housel wrote, 'Wealth is what you don't spend, which makes it invisible and hard to learn about by observing other people's lives. Spending is contagious; wealth is mysterious'. This really stuck with me, because being rich and being wealthy sound the same but they are different.

The rich need to spend money to show they are rich, whereas the wealthy need to keep their money to stay wealthy. Being wealthy is about saving your money, which buys time, allowing you to spend time doing the things you love.

This comes back to the concept that it's not about how much money you earn but rather how much you save. It's really important for your child to be able to practice living within their means. This is the complete opposite of living from pay cheque to pay cheque, with depleted bank accounts waiting for a new injection of cash. That's a stressful way to live, and research shows that financial stress has a direct link to depression and has a huge impact on a person's mental health.

Living within your means is all about spending only the money you have and not going into debt. It's about understanding wants versus needs and balancing the trade-offs between the two.

I think it's a good time to point out that we probably don't want our kids to grow up being cheap either. Cheapness focuses on spending as little as possible and prioritising price over quality or value. This is different to being frugal, which does take costs into consideration but also weighs up other considerations, such as value and long-term benefits.

Wealth isn't about being cheap and hoarding money; it's all about living a glorious life within your means.

Understanding their 'why'

There's a plethora of reasons why feeling as though you have a sense of purpose matters. It provides better health outcomes, less loneliness and more meaningfulness to a person's life. Having a sense of purpose can keep the long journey on track.

Just as we need to have a 'why' for our own goals and investments (which we discuss in chapter 7), so do our kids. Whether they have a financial goal of buying the latest Bluey toy or a first car, or donating a large sum to the local food bank, having a purpose for putting money away can motivate kids and keep them engaged.

You can set up milestones along the way to celebrate little accomplishments and focus on habits that are within their circle of control. This provides small dopamine hits along the way and sets the pace for a long-term goal (which can sometimes be demoralising if it takes a long time to achieve).

Discussing their goal and how they plan to achieve it, and even tracking it (via pen and paper or on a app), will help to keep them accountable while allowing you to support them in something that is really important to them – their very own 'why'.

Your biggest investment

These money foundations will ultimately prepare your child to go out into the real world. It's hard enough trying to navigate a job, rent, credit and super as is, but it's even more challenging when you don't have the financial literacy to make smart choices. Luckily, with your help, navigating the financial side of life will be a breeze for your kids because you instilled good money habits in them.

But money isn't the biggest investment you or your children can make.

The biggest investment anyone can make is in themselves.

You as a parent need to look after yourself. By ensuring that your health is in check, you are guaranteeing a healthier life for yourself. Make sure to exercise, get enough sleep, meditate and reduce your stress. By living a happy and healthy life, you are increasing your chance of being in your kid's life for a long time. So, look after you.

Yes, yes, our kids are also among our biggest investments. I mean, we wouldn't otherwise be spending hundreds of thousands of dollars on them during the course of their first 18 years of life! Therefore, it's important to remind them that, yes, they can invest in shares, ETFs and property, but their biggest investment should also be in themselves.

There are many ways our kids can invest in themselves, with education being the main way. This can inspire them to follow their interests, enabling them to grow into curious, passionate adults. With education, they become knowledgeable, well-rounded, inquisitive people. The wonderful thing is that no one can take their brains away from them. Support your child to excel in areas inside and outside of school that spark their interest, and to take on extracurricular activities that bring them happiness.

Lead by example. Teach them that you, too, are constantly learning, and it's okay to fail and take calculated risks. Help them to bounce back from setbacks and embrace new challenges, because this is all part of life and learning. Fostering a growth mindset helps kids learn grit and perseverance, which is important for when they start university and their first job or take on an entrepreneurial lifestyle. They are going to try new things, and they will make mistakes along the way, and it's important for us as parents to cheer them on and let them know that we are proud of them for trying, even in moments when things didn't work out the way they expected.

It's exciting to see who our kids will grow up to be, and surely, with your help, they will become independent, resilient, financially savvy little humans.

But what's most important is remembering that your kid looks up to you and wants to spend time with you. And as we know, time is finite. So embrace this special time. They are so lucky to have you. You are the best parent for your kid, and it's an honour for them to have you to teach and guide them to become the amazing young adult you always knew they could be.

And that's the best way you can set your child up for success.

Actionable steps

- Consider if an allowance is something that works for your family and how you plan to implement it.

- Attempt to use dinner time to talk about money in a casual way. Perhaps allocate a weekly night where you ask financial questions and support open, transparent discourse.

- Take time for yourself and make sure that you are investing in your own health and wellbeing. Write a list of things you can do to increase your wellness.

- Ensure you are supporting your children in their own interests through education, extracurricular activities or entrepreneurial endeavours. Remember that they are your biggest asset and you need to continue to empower them to make their own choices, learn from their mistakes and grow.

About the author

Hailing from Canada, Ana Kresina is the parent of two small children and a financial educator who works in the financial technology sector.

Her love of personal finance, parenthood and technology is apparent in both the content she creates documenting her journey to financial independence and in her role as Head of Product and Community at Pearler.

She is the co-host of one of Australia's leading podcasts, *Get Rich Slow Club*, and has been featured on the ABC and AusBiz TV, the *Girls That Invest* podcast and more.

In her free time, she loves to adventure, spend time with family and play board games. She's travelled to over 50 countries and now calls Australia home.

Resources

Introduction

AMP, 'New parents feel highest level of financial stress before baby', 24 September 2019, accessed 9 August 2023, corporate.amp.com.au/newsroom/2019/september/new-parents-feel-highest-level-of-financial-stress-before-baby-a.

Australian Bureau of Statistics, *Household and Families: Census*, 28 June 2022, abs.gov.au/statistics/people/people-and-communities/household-and-families-census/latest-release.

Qu, L & Baxter, J, 'Births in Australia', Australian Institute of Family Studies, accessed 9 August 2023, aifs.gov.au/research/facts-and-figures/births-australia-2023/.

Chapter 1 | Parenting money mindset

Alemany, L, Scarlata, M & Zacharakis, A, 'How the gender balance of investment teams shapes the risks they take', *Harvard Business Review*, 24 December 2020, hbr.org/2020/12/how-the-gender-balance-of-investment-teams-shapes-the-risks-they-take.

Clear, J, *Atomic Habits*, Random House UK, London, 2018.

Cronqvist, H & Siegel, S, 'The Origins of Savings Behavior: AFA 2011 Denver Meetings Paper', *SSRN*, 7 November 2013.

Killingsworth, MA, 'Experienced well-being rises with income, even above $75,000 per year', *PNAS*, vol. 118, no. 4, 2021, e2016976118.

Killingsworth, MA, Kahneman, D & Mellers, B, 'Income and emotional well-being: A conflict resolved', *PNAS*, vol. 120, no. 10, 2023, e2208661120.

Lindenfeld Hall, S, 'How to Retire Early Even If You Have Kids', *Parents*, 19 January 2021, parents.com/parenting/money/saving/how-to-retire-early-even-if-you-have-kids/.

M Housel, *The Psychology of Money: Timeless lessons on wealth, greed, and happiness*, Harriman House Publishing, Hampshire, 2020.

Maurer, T, 'Why women are better (investors) than men', *Forbes*, 30 April 2023, forbes.com/sites/timmaurer/2023/04/30/why-women-are-better-investors-than-men/?sh=48b414d6799d.

McGowan, SK & Behar, E, 'A preliminary investigation of stimulus control training for worry: Effects on anxiety and insomnia', *Behavior Modification*, vol. 37, no. 1, 2013, pp. 90–112.

McKinson, F, 'What does the gay wage gap mean for LGBTQ+ families?', *Parents*, 16 June 2021, parents.com/parenting/money/lgbtq-equal-pay-day-wage-gap/.

Morin, A, '2 psychological tricks that will help you stop worrying about things you can't control', *Forbes*, 11 May 2020, forbes.com/sites/amymorin/2020/05/11/2-psychological-tricks-that-will-help-you-stop-worrying-about-things-you-cant-control/.

Troller-Renfree, SV, Costanzo, MA, Duncan, GJ, Magnuson, K, Gennetian, LA, Yoshikawa, H, Halpern-Meekin S, Fox, NA & Noble, KG, 'The impact of a poverty reduction intervention on infant brain activity', *PNAS*, vol. 119, no. 5, 2022, e2115649119.

Whitebread, D & Bingham, S, *Habit Formation and Learning in Young Children*, The Money Advice Service, May 2013, mascdn.azureedge.net/cms/the-money-advice-service-habit-formation-and-learning-in-young-children-may2013.pdf.

Your Financial Wellness, 'Financial wellness matters', accessed 2 August 2023, yourfinancialwellness.com.au/_about/Research.aspx.

Chapter 2 | Getting your finances in order before kids

The Association of Superannuation Funds of Australia, 'ASFA retirement standard', accessed 3 August 2023, superannuation.asn.au/resources/retirement-standard.

Australian Banking Association, 'Open banking', accessed 2 August 2023, ausbanking.org.au/priorities/open-banking/.

Australian Bureau of Statistics, 'Employee earnings', 14 December 2022, abs.gov.au/statistics/labour/earnings-and-working-conditions/employee-earnings/latest-release.

Australian Bureau of Statistics, 'Household income and wealth, Australia', 28 April 2022, abs.gov.au/statistics/economy/finance/household-income-and-wealth-australia/latest-release.

Australian Bureau of Statistics, 'Same-sex couples in Australia, 2016', *Census of Population and Housing: Reflecting Australia – Stories from the Census, 2016*, 18 January 2018, abs.gov.au/ausstats/abs@.nsf/Lookup/2071.0main+features852016.

Australian Institute of Business, 'Changing jobs – how often is too often?', 4 April 2023, aib.edu.au/blog/career-development/changing-jobs-how-often-is-too-often/.

Australian Retirement Trust, 'Average super balance by age', accessed 3 August 2023, australianretirementtrust.com.au/superannuation/how-much-super-should-i-have.

Australian Taxation Office, 'Lost and unclaimed super by postcode', 18 March 2021, ato.gov.au/About-ATO/Research-and-statistics/In-detail/Super-statistics/Super-accounts-data/Lost-and-unclaimed-super-by-postcode/.

Australian Taxation Office, 'Medicare levy reduction – family income', 23 June 2023, ato.gov.au/Individuals/Medicare-and-private-health-insurance/Medicare-levy/Medicare-levy-reduction/Medicare-levy-reduction---family-income.

Australian Taxation Office, 'Medicare levy reduction for low-income earners', 3 July 2023, ato.gov.au/Individuals/Medicare-and-private-health-insurance/Medicare-levy/Medicare-levy-reduction/Medicare-levy-reduction-for-low-income-earners.

Australian Taxation Office, 'Medicare levy surcharge income, thresholds and rates', 3 April 2023, ato.gov.au/Individuals/Medicare-and-private-health-insurance/Medicare-levy-surcharge/Medicare-levy-surcharge-income,-thresholds-and-rates.

Brittle, Z, 'When three's not the charm: How to manage the higher risk of divorce when baby comes along', *The Washington Post*, 30 June 2015, washingtonpost.com/news/inspired-life/wp/2015/06/30/when-threes-not-the-charm-how-to-manage-the-higher-risk-of-divorce-when-baby-comes-along/.

Centre for Future Work, 'Women Earn $1m less than men & $136,000 less in super over working life', 8 March 2023, futurework.org.au/post/women-earn-1m-less-than-men-136000-less-in-super-over-working-life.

Cooley, PL, Hubbard, CM & Walz, DT. 'Retirement savings: choosing a withdrawal rate that is sustainable', *AII Journal*, February 1998, pp. 16-21, aaii.com/journal/199802/feature.pdf.

Doss, BD & Rhoades, GK, 'The transition to parenthood: Impact on couples' romantic relationships', *Current Opinion in Psychology*, vol. 13, 2017, pp. 25-28.

Family Relationships Online, 'Family Relationships Online', accessed 2 August 2023, familyrelationships.gov.au.

Fitzsimmons, C, 'Financial stress is big cause of break-ups. How to money-proof your relationship', *Sydney Morning Herald*, 8 September 2017, smh.com.au/money/planning-and-budgeting/financial-stress-is-big-cause-of-breakups-how-to-moneyproof-your-relationship-20170908-gydyc5.html.

The Gottman Institute, 'Parenting', accessed 2 August 2023, gottman.com/about/research/parenting/.

The Gottman Institute, 'Same-Sex Couples', accessed 2 August 2023, gottman.com/ about/research/same-sex-couples/.

Jimenez Law Firm, 'What percent of marriages end in divorce because of money?', 29 December 2022, thejimenezlawfirm.com/what-percent-of-marriages-end-in-divorce-because-of-money/.

Kahnman, D, Krueger, AB, Sckade, DA, Schwarz, N & Stone, AA, 'A survey method for characterizing daily life experience: The day reconstruction method', *Science*, vol. 306, no. 5702, 2004, pp. 1776–1780.

Mr. Money Mustache, 'The shockingly simple math behind early retirement', 13 January 2012, mrmoneymustache.com/2012/01/13/the-shockingly-simple-math-behind-early-retirement/.

Nelson, SK, Kushlev, K, & Lyubomirsky, S, 'The pains and pleasures of parenting: When, why, and how is parenthood associated with more or less well-being?', *Psychological Bulletin*, vol. 140, no. 3, 2014, pp. 846–895.

PostpartumDepression.org, 'Postpartum depression statistics', accessed 2 August 2023, postpartumdepression.org/resources/statistics/.

Pape, S, *The Barefoot Investor*, Wiley, Milton, 2016.

Services Australia, 'Meeting the income test', 1 July 2023, servicesaustralia.gov.au/meeting-income-test-for-parental-leave-pay-for-child-born-or-adopted-from-1-july-2023.

Wilkins, R, Vera-Toscano, E, Botha, F, Wooden, M & Trinh, T-A, *The Household, Income and Labour Dynamics in Australia Survey: Selected Findings from Waves 1 to 20: The 17th Annual Statistical Report of the HILDA Survey*, The Melbourne Institute, 2022, melbourneinstitute.unimelb. edu.au/__data/assets/pdf_file/0011/4382057/HILDA_Statistical_Report_ 2022.pdf.

Chapter 3 | The cost of having kids

Australian Competition & Consumer Commission, 'Pricing practices and operating costs of childcare services to be examined, as latest ACCC report confirms fees outpaced inflation', 5 July 2023, accc.gov.au/media-release/ pricing-practices-and-operating-costs-of-childcare-services-to-be-examined-as-latest-accc-report-confirms-fees-outpaced-inflation.

Australian Competition & Consumer Commission, *Childcare inquiry: Interim report, Commonwealth of Australia*, June 2023, accc.gov.au/system/ files/Childcare%20inquiry%20-%20Interim%20report%20-%20June%20 2023_0.pdf.

Australian Energy Regulator, 'Comparison tools', accessed 9 August 2023, aer.gov.au/consumers/switching-retailers/comparison-tools#energy-made-easy.

Australian Institute of Family Studies, 'New estimates of the costs of children', accessed 9 August 2023, aifs.gov.au/research/family-matters/no-100/new-estimates-costs-children.

Barnett, KB, 'My mommy tax: six months of nursing cost more than a year of formula', *The Guardian*, 2 February 2016, theguardian.com/ commentisfree/2016/feb/02/my-mommy-tax-six-months-of-nursing-cost-more-than-a-year-of-formula.

Browne, R, 'Housework twice the burden for women', *The Sydney Morning Herald*, 17 May 2013, smh.com.au/opinion/housework-twice-the-burden-for-women-20130516-2jpc4.html.

Carsales staff, 'Which Australian states offer the best EV incentives?', *Carsales*, 14 June 2023, carsales.com.au/editorial/details/which-australian-states-offer-the-best-ev-incentives-131927/.

Choosi, *The Choosi Cost of Kids Report 2023*, February 2023, choosi.com. au/documents/the-cost-of-kids-report-whitepaper.pdf.

Department of Environment, Land, Water and Planning, 'Victorian Energy Compare', accessed 9 August 2023, compare.energy.vic.gov.au.

Energy Made Easy, 'Find the right energy plan for you', accessed 9 August 2023, energymadeeasy.gov.au.

Erem, C, 'Aussie parents are spending $1,859 on average for extracurricular activities, says Mozo', *Mozo*, 31 January 2020, mozo.com.au/family-finances/aussie-parents-are-spending-1-859-on-average-for-extracurricular-activities-says-mozo.

Field, N, 'How much does it cost to have a baby in Australia?', *Canstar*, 8 March 2023, canstar.com.au/health-insurance/how-to-afford-a-baby/.

Finder, *Finder's Parenting Report 2021*, October 2021, dvh1deh6tagwk.cloudfront.net/finder-au/wp-uploads/2021/09/Finders-Parenting-Report.pdf.

Futurity Investment Group, 'Cost of education in Australia in 2023', accessed 3 August 2023, futurityinvest.com.au/insights/futurity-blog/2023/02/01/cost-of-education-in-australia-in-2023?_ga=2.79281684.1057576875.1683195887-723701853.1682313060.

Futurity Investment Group, 'School fees in Australia: a full breakdown', accessed 3 August 2023, futurityinvest.com.au/insights/futurity-blog/2022/04/27/school-fees-australia.

Futurity Investment Group, *Schooling in Australia: Exploring the financial impact of providing a quality education*, 2023, drive.google.com/file/d/1TmE IgZGWQdQ20JQwpBgJ7AiB3PNxPmnF/view.

Gattuso, R, 'Why LGBTQ couples split household tasks more equally', *BBC*, 11 March 2021, bbc.com/worklife/article/20210309-why-lgbtq-couples-split-household-tasks-more-equally.

Grace Papers, 'Mums working longer hours than CEOs', 1 April 2021, gracepapers.com.au/mums-working-longer-hours-than-ceos/.

Haiek, C, 'Mum-approved advice for keeping your baby warm and safe on cold nights', *news.com.au*, 9 June 2020, kidspot.com.au/parenting/primary-school/how-to-keep-your-baby-warm-and-safe-on-cold-nights/news-story/5d583f265a36a729b3fd80957e6585de.

Hams, S, 'Nappy recycling program to reduce plastic waste in landfill harvests tonnes within months', *ABC News*, 7 December 2022, abc.net.au/news/2022-12-07/nappy-recycling-program-to-reduce-plastic-waste-in-landfill/101737628.

Hitch, G, 'New multiple-birth grant recommended to ease unexpected costs facing families of multiples', *ABC News*, 20 March 2023, abc.net.au/news/2023-03-20/twins-triplets-multiple-births-call-more-financial-help-budget/102098222.

IVFAustralia, 'IVF treatment costs', accessed 3 August 2023, ivf.com.au/ivf-cost/ivf-costs.

Jenkins, C, 'Working mums use holiday time to care for kids with colds and flu', *news.com.au*, 27 June 2017, news.com.au/lifestyle/health/health-problems/working-mums-use-holiday-time-to-care-for-kids-with-colds-and-flu/news-story/f901270e6896a19877e3988102a6e3e5.

Kwiet-Evans, N, 'Private school exodus: Families exit expensive schools as cost of living soars', *Finder*, 10 January 2023, finder.com.au/families-exit-private-schools-2023.

Merrill, 'The financial journey of modern parenting: Joy, complexity and sacrifice', *Life Stage Series: Parenting*, Bank of America Corporation, 2020, mlaem.fs.ml.com/content/dam/ml/registration/ml_parentstudybrochure.pdf.

Mihm, U & Ciaramidaro, R, 'How to buy the best disposable and cloth nappies', *Choice*, 8 October 2020, choice.com.au/babies-and-kids/baby-clothes-and-nappies/nappies/buying-guides/disposable-and-cloth-nappies.

Mihm, U & Smith, G, 'The cost of having a baby – and how to budget for it', *Choice*, 8 October 2020, choice.com.au/babies-and-kids/getting-ready-for-baby/planning-for-baby/articles/budgeting-for-baby.

Murtaugh, PA & Schlax, MG, 'Reproduction and the carbon legacies of individuals', *Global Environmental Change*, vol. 19, no. 1, 2009, pp. 14-20.

Nelson, A, 'The politics of breastfeeding (and why it must change)', *Forbes*, 24 October 2018, forbes.com/sites/amynelson1/2018/10/24/the-politics-of-breastfeeding-and-why-it-must-change/?sh=68ad38193163.

NSW Government, 'Costs', accessed 3 August 2023, nsw.gov.au/having-children/adopting-a-child/costs.

The Office of the Fair Work Ombudsman, 'Paid sick and carer's leave', accessed 3 August 2023, fairwork.gov.au/leave/sick-and-carers-leave/paid-sick-and-carers-leave.

The Office of the Fair Work Ombudsman, 'Unpaid carer's leave', accessed 3 August 2023, fairwork.gov.au/leave/sick-and-carers-leave/unpaid-carers-leave.

Payne, H, 'Stop cooking with gas, for asthma's sake', *The Medical Republic*, 7 December 2022, medicalrepublic.com.au/stop-cooking-with-gas-for-asthmas-sake/82960.

Phillips, B, Li, J, Taylor, M, 2013, *Cost of Kids: The cost of raising children in Australia: AMP.NATSEM Income and Wealth Report, no. 33*, AMP, May 2013, goldsborough.com.au/assets/publication-files/AMP-NATSEM.pdf.

Płotka-Wasylka, J, Makoś-Chełstowska, P, Kurowska-Susdorf, A, Treviño, MJS, Guzmán, SZ, Mostafa, H & Cordella M, 'End-of-life management of single-use baby diapers: Analysis of technical, health and environment aspects', *Science of The Total Environment*, vol. 836, 2022, 155339.

Rewiring Australia, 'Electrify everything', accessed 3 August 2023, rewiringaustralia.org/.

Statista, 'Baby & Child – Australia', 2023, statista.com/outlook/cmo/beauty-personal-care/skin-care/baby-child/australia?currency=AUD.

Stewart, E, 'Cloth nappies or disposables? We crunched the numbers so you don't have to', *ABC News*, 25 February 2020, abc.net.au/news/2020-02-25/cloth-nappies-vs-disposables-crunching-the-numbers/11994864.

Stewart, E, 'The cost of childbirth and the hidden bills to prepare for', *ABC Everyday*, 18 October 2018, abc.net.au/everyday/the-cost-of-childbirth-and-the-hidden-bills-to-prepare-for/10350778.

Sudarshan, S, 'Back to school costs 2023', *Finder*, 3 January 2023, finder.com.au/back-to-school-costs.

Suncorp, 'The rising cost of kids', *Suncorp Newsroom*, 17 December 2021, suncorpgroup.com.au/news/news/cost-of-kids-2021.

Suncorp, *Suncorp Bank Cost of Kids Report*, 2021, suncorpgroup.com.au/uploads/Suncorp-Bank-2021-Cost-of-Kids-Report.pdf.

UNSW Media, 'Almost one in 20 babies in Australia born through IVF', *UNSW Sydney Newsroom*, 6 September 2020, newsroom.unsw.edu.au/news/health/almost-one-20-babies-australia-born-through-ivf.

Chapter 4 | Preparing for parental leave

Amanatullah, ET, & Morris, MW, 'Negotiating gender roles: Gender differences in assertive negotiating are mediated by women's fear of backlash and attenuated when negotiating on behalf of others', *Journal of Personality and Social Psychology*, vol. 98, no. 2, 2010, pp. 256–267.

Artz, B, Goodall, AH, & Oswald, AJ, 'Do women ask?', *Industrial Relations*, vol. 57, no. 4, 2018, pp. 611–636.

The Association of Superannuation Funds of Australia, 'ASFA calls on Government to close retirement savings gender gap', 7 March 2023, superannuation.asn.au/media/media-releases/2023/media-release-7-march-2023.

Australian Taxation Office, 'Contribution caps', 2 August 2022, ato.gov.au/Super/Self-managed-super-funds/Contributions-and-rollovers/Contribution-caps.

Australian Taxation Office, 'Contributions splitting', 5 August 2019, ato.gov.au/Forms/Contributions-splitting.

Australian Unions, 'Maternity leave', Australian Council of Trade Unions, accessed 7 August 2023, australianunions.org.au/factsheet/maternity-leave/.

Bernelf, F, 'Same sex parental leave: Legislation and equality', Umea University [thesis], 2017, diva-portal.org/smash/get/diva2:1220717/FULLTEXT01.pdf.

Bowles, HR, Babcock, L, & Lai, L, 'Social incentives for gender differences in the propensity to initiate negotiations: Sometimes it does hurt to ask', *Organizational Behavior and Human Decision Processes*, vol. 103, no. 1, 2007, pp. 84–103.

Brown, S, 'Women-owned business and mom-owned business statistics', *Mompowerment*, 10 May 2023, mompowerment.com/small-business-and-mompreneur-statistics.

Centre for Future Work, 'Women Earn $1m less than men & $136,000 less in super over working life', 8 March 2023, futurework.org.au/post/women-earn-1m-less-than-men-136000-less-in-super-over-working-life.

Circle In, 'The Fatherhood Trap: Why Australian Dads Want To Take Parental Leave But Don't (Or Can't)', accessed 7 August 2023, circlein.com/research-and-guides/the-fatherhood-trap/.

Cunningham, K, '"A no-brainer": Paying attention early can supercharge your super', *The Guardian*, 4 April 2023, theguardian.com/australia-news/2023/apr/04/a-no-brainer-paying-attention-early-can-supercharge-your-super.

Diamond, R, 'The motherhood penalty in the workplace', *Psychology Today*, 13 February 2023, psychologytoday.com/au/blog/preparing-for-parenthood/202302/the-motherhood-penalty-in-the-workplace.

Fair Work Ombudsman, 'Our role and purpose', accessed 7 August 2023, fairwork.gov.au/about-us/our-role-and-purpose.

Finder, *International Women's Day 2022: Work, wealth and financial equality*, March 2022, dvh1deh6tagwk.cloudfront.net/finder-au/wp-uploads/2022/03/International-Womens-Day-2022.pdf.

Gromada, A, & Richardson, D, *Where do rich countries stand on childcare*, UNICEF, June 2021, unicef-irc.org/publications/pdf/where-do-rich-countries-stand-on-childcare.pdf.

Huang, J, Krivkovich, A, Rambachan, I & Yee, L, 'For mothers in the workplace, a year (and counting) like no other', *McKinsey & Company*, 5 May 2021, mckinsey.com/featured-insights/diversity-and-inclusion/for-mothers-in-the-workplace-a-year-and-counting-like-no-other.

Levanon, A, England, P, & Allison, P, 'Occupational feminization and pay: Assessing causal dynamics using 1950–2000 U.S. census data', *Social Forces*, vol. 88, no. 2, 2009, pp. 865–891.

Liner, E, 'A dollar short: What's holding women back from equal pay?', *Third Way*, 18 March 2016, thirdway.org/report/a-dollar-short-whats-holding-women-back-from-equal-pay.

Mercy Foundation, 'Older women and homelessness', accessed 7 August 2023, mercyfoundation.com.au/our-focus/ending-homelessness/older-women-and-homelessness/.

Merrill, 'The financial journey of modern parenting: Joy, complexity and sacrifice', *Life Stage Series: Parenting*, Bank of America Corporation, 2020, mlaem.fs.ml.com/content/dam/ml/registration/ml_parentstudybrochure.pdf.

Miller, CC, 'As women take over a male-dominated field, the pay drops', *The New York Times*, 18 March 2016, nytimes.com/2016/03/20/upshot/as-women-take-over-a-male-dominated-field-the-pay-drops.html.

Organisation for Economic Co-operation and Development (OECD), 'Parental leave: Where are the fathers?', *Policy Brief*, March 2016, oecd.org/gender/parental-leave-where-are-the-fathers.pdf.

Reif, J, Kunz, F, Kugler, K, & Brodbeck, F, 'Negotiation contexts: How and why they shape women's and men's decision to negotiate', *Negotiation and Conflict Management Research*, vol. 12, no.4, 2019, pp. 343–366.

Services Australia, 'Family Tax Benefit', 25 January 2023, servicesaustralia. gov.au/family-tax-benefit.

Services Australia, 'If you're self-employed and work on a Parental Leave Pay day', 27 March 2023, servicesaustralia.gov.au/if-youre-self-employed-and-work-day-parental-leave-pay-for-child-born-or-adopted-from-1-july-2023?context=64479.

Services Australia, 'Meeting the income test', 1 July 2023, servicesaustralia. gov.au/meeting-income-test-for-parental-leave-pay-for-child-born-or-adopted-from-1-july-2023.

Services Australia, 'Parental Leave Pay for a child born or adopted from 1 July 2023', 1 July 2023, servicesaustralia.gov.au/parental-leave-pay-for-child-born-or-adopted-from-1-july-2023.

Services Australia, 'Self-employed parents', 27 March 2023, servicesaustralia.gov.au/self-employed-parents-work-test-for-parental-leave-pay-for-child-born-or-adopted-before-1-july-2023.

Services Australia, 'Work requirements', 1 July 2023, servicesaustralia.gov. au/work-requirements-for-parental-leave-pay-for-child-born-or-adopted-from-1-july-2023.

Sharples, S, '"Horrible": Why we need to change this appalling reality', *news.com.au*, 2 May 2022, news.com.au/finance/superannuation/horrible-why-we-need-to-change-this-appalling-reality/news-story/d55450af595d61eddde0f13bb7f632a5.

Stewart, E, 'Should you hide the bump? What to consider when buying a home', *ABC News*, 10 February 2022, abc.net.au/news/2022-02-10/home-loan-bank-pregnancy-starting-a-family/100815070.

Tindall, S, 'How to pause your mortgage repayments during pregnancy', *Money*, 16 January 2019, moneymag.com.au/pause-mortgage-payments-pregnancy.

Voidonicolas, R, 'The real post-pandemic boom: Mom entrepreneurs', *Shopify*, 21 March 2023, shopify.com/blog/mom-entrepreneurs.

Walsh, E, 'Fathers and parental Leave', *Australian Institute of Family Studies*, May 2019, aifs.gov.au/resources/short-articles/fathers-and-parental-leave.

Winter, V, 'Multiple Centrelink payments are increasing today. Here's which ones are going up and by how much', *ABC News*, 20 March 2023, abc.net.au/news/2023-03-20/centrelink-increases-jobseeker-pension-indexation-inflation/102104316.

Wood, D, Emslie, O, & Griffiths, K, *Day days: How more gender-equal parental leave could improve the lives of Australian families*, Grattan Institute, September 2021, grattan.edu.au/wp-content/uploads/2021/09/Dad-Days-Grattan-Institute-Report.pdf.

Wootton, H, 'These "two simple measures" would close super gender gap by 2050', *Australian Financial Review*, 8 March 2023, afr.com/policy/tax-and-super/two-simple-measures-would-close-super-gender-gap-by-2050-20230308-p5cqgy.

Workplace Gender Equality Agency, 'Australian employers paying up for mums and dads on parental leave', 8 February 2022, wgea.gov.au/newsroom/parental-leave-scorecard.

Workplace Gender Equality Agency, 'Media Release: National gender pay gap of 13.3% just a fraction of the real cost on women', February 2022, wgea.gov.au/newsroom/media-release-national-gender-pay-gap-february-2023.

Workplace Gender Equality Agency, *Developing a Leading Practice Parental Leave Policy: A guide for employers*, February 2022, wgea.gov.au/sites/default/files/documents/WGEA-Leading-Practice-Parental-Leave-Policy-Guide.pdf.

Yu, W-H, & Hara, Y, 'Motherhood penalties and fatherhood premiums: Effects of parenthood on earnings growth within and across firms', *Demography*, vol. 58, no. 1, 2021, pp. 247–272.

Chapter 5 | Navigating early childhood education and care

Australian Children's Education & Care Quality Authority, '89% of children's education and care services meeting or exceeding standards', 4 May 2023, acecqa.gov.au/latest-news/89-childrens-education-and-care-services-meeting-or-exceeding-standards-0.

Australian Competition & Consumer Commission, 'Pricing practices and operating costs of childcare services to be examined, as latest ACCC report confirms fees outpaced inflation', 5 July 2023, accc.gov.au/media-release/pricing-practices-and-operating-costs-of-childcare-services-to-be-examined-as-latest-accc-report-confirms-fees-outpaced-inflation.

Centre for Policy Development, *Starting Better: A guarantee for young children and families*, Centre for Policy Development, November 2021, cpd.org.au/wp-content/uploads/2021/11/CPD-Starting-Better-Report.pdf.

Curtis, K, 'Focus on childcare bottom dollar leads to more safety breaches, report finds', *The Sydney Morning Herald*, 6 October 2021, smh.com.au/politics/federal/focus-on-childcare-bottom-dollar-leads-to-more-safety-breaches-report-finds-20211005-p58x9a.html.

Duffy, C & Branley, A, 'Childcare subsidies are increasing, but inflation and fee hikes will take a bite', *ABC News*, 3 July 2023, abc.net.au/news/2023-07-03/centrelink-rules-and-childcare-subsidy-changes-how-much-benefit/102510374.

Early Childhood Australia, 'The key reasons why early learning matters', *The Spoke*, 17 October 2022, thespoke.earlychildhoodaustralia.org.au/key-reasons-early-learning-matters/.

Gromada, A, & Richardson, D, *Where do rich countries stand on childcare?*, UNICEF, June 2021, unicef-irc.org/publications/pdf/where-do-rich-countries-stand-on-childcare.pdf.

Hurley, P, 'Childcare deserts & oases: How accessible is childcare in Australia?', *Victoria University*, 22 March 2022, vu.edu.au/mitchell-institute/early-learning/childcare-deserts-oases-how-accessible-is-childcare-in-australia.

Hutchens, G, 'Meet the millions of people who aren't employed, who aren't considered "unemployed"', *ABC News*, 31 October 2021, abc.net.au/news/2021-10-31/meet-the-millions-of-people-who-are-not-employed/100582656.

Impact Economics and Policy, *Child Care Subsidy Activity Test: Undermining child development and parental participation*, Impact Economics and Policy, August 2022, static1.squarespace.com/static/61e32e62c8c8337e6fd7a1e6/t/630de5c741a8de08ad48d593/1661855185396/Undermining+Child+Development+And+Parental+Participation+Report_FINAL.pdf.

Indeed Editorial Team, '20 lowest-paid jobs in Australia (with salary information)', *Indeed*, 20 July 2023, au.indeed.com/career-advice/finding-a-job/lowest-paid-jobs-in-australia.

Le Baron, V, 'The psychological benefits of daycare on toddlers', *Kidspot*, 15 May 2018, kidspot.com.au/parenting/preschool/the-psychological-benefits-of-daycare-on-toddlers/news-story/f357bed4d3a2ffc3dfb3fb5ddacc4cc8.

Lucas, F, 'ECEC job advertisement have doubled since COVID-19, illustrating the depth of staffing crisis', *The Sector*, 31 May 2022, thesector.com.au/2022/05/31/ecec-job-advertisements-have-doubled-since-covid-19-illustrating-the-depth-of-staffing-crisis/.

The Morning Show, 'Australia's childcare costs: How we compare to the rest of the world', *7News*, 4 June 2019, 7news.com.au/the-morning-show/australias-childcare-costs-how-we-compare-to-the-rest-of-the-world-c-146357.

Only About Children, 'Childcare Subsidy Information (CCS)', accessed 8 August 2023, oac.edu.au/for-families/child-subsidy-information/.

Rogers, M, 'Early educators around the world feel burnt out and devalued. Here's how we can help', *The Conversation*, 18 April 2023, theconversation.com/early-educators-around-the-world-feel-burnt-out-and-devalued-heres-how-we-can-help-202513.

Rogers, M, Boyd, W & Sims, M, 'Smile and wave ladies: The attempt to silence Grace Tame mirrors the plight of early childhood educators', *Women's Agenda*, 2 February 2023, womensagenda.com.au/latest/smile-and-wave-ladies-the-attempts-to-silence-grace-tame-mirrors-the-plight-of-early-childhood-educators/.

Services Australia, 'Additional child care subsidy', Australian Government, 10 December 2021, servicesaustralia.gov.au/additional-child-care-subsidy.

Services Australia, 'Child care subsidy', 18 July 2023, servicesaustralia.gov.au/child-care-subsidy.

Services Australia, 'How to claim', 24 January 2023, servicesaustralia.gov.au/how-to-claim-child-care-subsidy.

Services Australia, 'If your child is absent from child care', 5 July 2023, servicesaustralia.gov.au/child-care-subsidy-if-your-child-absent-from-child-care?context=41186.

Starting Blocks, 'Brain development in children', accessed 8 August 2023, startingblocks.gov.au/other-resources/factsheets/brain-development-in-children.

Starting Blocks, 'Child care subsidy calculator', accessed 8 August 2023, startingblocks.gov.au/child-care-subsidy-calculator.

Warrilow, P, Graham, N & Robertson, C, *Not-for-profit Education and Care: High quality, accessible and resilient*, Australian Community Children's Services, May 2021, ausccs.org.au/wp-content/uploads/2021/08/TICCS_2021_wave6.pdf.

Winter, V, 'Multiple Centrelink payments are increasing today. Here's which ones are going up and by how much', *ABC News*, 20 March 2023, abc.net.au/news/2023-03-20/centrelink-increases-jobseeker-pension-indexation-inflation/102104316.

Wood, D, Griffiths, K & Ermslie, O, *Cheaper Childcare: A practical plan to boost female workforce participation*, Grattan Institute, August 2020, grattan.edu.au/wp-content/uploads/2020/08/Cheaper-Childcare-Grattan-Institute-Report.pdf.

Chapter 6 | Investing for your family's future: Investing explained

Australian Prudential Regulation Authority, 'Financial claims scheme', accessed 9 August 2023, apra.gov.au/financial-claims-scheme-0.

Merrill, 'The financial journey of modern parenting: Joy, complexity and sacrifice', *Life Stage Series: Parenting*, Bank of America Corporation, 2020, mlaem.fs.ml.com/content/dam/ml/registration/ml_parentstudybrochure.pdf.

Moneysmart, 'Property schemes', accessed 9 August 2023, https://moneysmart.gov.au/property-investment/property-schemes.

Sullivan, B & Curry, B, 'Average stock market return', *Forbes*, 16 February 2023, forbes.com/advisor/investing/average-stock-market-return/.

Udland, M, 'Fidelity reviewed which investors did best and what they found was hilarious', *Business Insider*, 5 September 2014, businessinsider.com/forgetful-investors-performed-best-2014-9.

Wasik, JF, 'How Buffett won his $1 million bet', *Forbes*, 8 January 2018, forbes.com/sites/johnwasik/2018/01/08/how-buffett-won-his-1-million-bet.

Chapter 7 | Investing for kids

Australian Taxation Office, 'Conditions of release', accessed 9 August 2023, ato.gov.au/Super/APRA-regulated-funds/Paying-benefits/Releasing-benefits/Conditions-of-release/.

Australian Taxation Office, 'Excess contributions tax and how funds report your contributions', accessed 9 August 2023, ato.gov.au/Individuals/Super/In-detail/Withdrawing-and-using-your-super/Excess-contributions-tax-and-how-funds-report-your-contributions/?page=10.

Australian Taxation Office, 'First home super saver scheme', accessed 9 August 2023, ato.gov.au/Individuals/Super/Withdrawing-and-using-your-super/First-Home-Super-Saver-Scheme/.

Australian Taxation Office, 'Growing your super', accessed 9 August 2023, ato.gov.au/Individuals/Super/Growing-and-keeping-track-of-your-super/Growing-your-super/.

Australian Taxation Office, 'Tax rates if you're under 18 years old', accessed 9 August 2023, ato.gov.au/rates/Tax-rates-if-you-re-under-18-years-old/.

Finder, *Finder's Parenting Report 2021*, October 2021, dvh1deh6tagwk.cloudfront.net/finder-au/wp-uploads/2021/09/Finders-Parenting-Report.pdf.

Jacobs, D, 'Warren Buffet's net worth over the years', *FinMasters*, 3 July 2023, finmasters.com/warren-buffett-net-worth/.

Jocum, M, 'What you need to know when considering investment bonds (insurance bonds)', *Stockspot*, 22 May 2023, blog.stockspot.com.au/investment-bonds.

Treasury, *Better Targeted Superannuation Concessions: Consultation paper*, 31 March 2023, ato.gov.au/Individuals/Super/Growing-and-keeping-track-of-your-super/Growing-your-super/.

Wootton, H & Dean, L, ''Retirees giving their kids cash as super drawdowns increase', *Australian Financial Review*, 30 June 2023, afr.com/policy/tax-and-super/retirees-giving-their-kids-cash-as-super-drawdowns-increase-20230623-p5diyx.

Chapter 8 | How to set up your kid for financial success

Australian Council for Educational Research, 'No gender gap in Australian student financial literacy: PISA', 21 July 2020, acer.org/au/discover/article/no-gender-gap-in-Australian-student-financial-literacy-pisa.

Bavin, E, 'Aussies spend $8.6 million every day on credit card debt', *Yahoo Finance AU*, 9 May 2023, au.news.yahoo.com/aussies-spend-86-million-every-day-on-credit-card-debt-002458034.html.

Berger, A, Tzur, G & Posner, MI, 'Infant brains detect arithmetic errors', *PNAS*, vol. 103, no. 33, 2006, pp. 12649-12653.

Borman, S, 'Australia's best personal loans for August 2023', *Mozo*, 1 August 2023, mozo.com.au/best/best-personal-loans.

Brower, T, 'The power of purpose and why it matters now', *Forbes*, 22 August 2021, forbes.com/sites/tracybrower/2021/08/22/the-power-of-purpose-and-why-it-matters-now/.

Cooke, G, 'Australian credit card and debit card statistics', *Finder*, 10 July 2023, finder.com.au/credit-cards/credit-card-statistics.

de Zwaan, L & West, T, *Financial Literacy of Young Australians: What they know, what they don't know, and what we can do to help*, Financial Basics Foundation, March 2022, financialbasics.org.au/uploads/media/documents/FBF%20Financial%20Literacy%20of%20Young%20Australians%20March%202022.pdf.

Dean, L, 'Most Australians can't answer all of these five basic money questions', *Australian Financial Review*, 5 December 2022, afr.com/wealth/personal-finance/most-australians-can-t-answer-all-of-these-five-basic-money-questions-20221130-p5c2kv.

Derhy, M, '"Research has shown that doing something kind for someone else can make us happier" With Author Dr. Kate Mihevc Edwards and Marco Derhy', *Authority Magazine*, 26 November 2018, medium.com/authority-magazine/research-has-shown-that-doing-something-kind-for-someone-else-can-make-us-happier-with-author-dr-cbcb33f4d7ce.

Dituri, P, Davidson, A & Marley-Payne, J, 'Combining financial education with mathematics coursework: Findings from a pilot study', *Journal of Financial Counseling and Planning*, vol. 30, no. 2, 2019.

Earp, J, 'Infographic: Financial education in schools', *Australian Council for Educational Research*, 3 April 2023, research.acer.edu.au/teacher_graphics/160/.

Fernando, J, 'Time value of money explained with formula and examples', *Investopedia*, 28 March 2023, investopedia.com/terms/t/timevalueofmoney.asp.

Foulkes, L, Leung, JT, Knoll, LJ & Blakemore, S-J, 'Age differences in the prosocial influence effect', *Developmental Science*, vol.21, no. 6, 2018, e12666.

Hoffower, H, 'Millennials might lag behind their parents when it comes to money, but there's something they do better: talk about it', *Business Insider*, 1 November 2019, businessinsider.com/personal-finance/millennials-more-open-discussing-money-finances-than-boomers-2019-10.

Housel, M, 'After the fact', *Collab Fund*, 8 February 2022, collabfund.com/blog/after-the-fact/.

Jackson Curran, E, '7 science-based benefits of eating together as a family', *Parents*, 12 February 2023, parents.com/recipes/tips/unexpected-benefits-of-eating-together-as-a-family-according-to-science/.

Kahneman, D & Tversky, A, 'Prospect theory: An analysis of decision under risk', *Econometrica*, vol. 47, no. 2, 1979, pp. 263–292.

Kramer, P, 'Teaching kids the value of money', *Parents*, 10 October 2019, parents.com/parenting/money/family-finances/teaching-kids-value-of-money.

Loudenback, T, 'A survey of 2,000 Americans found they're more likely to talk about politics and relationships with their friends than money', *Business Insider*, 17 June 2021, businessinsider.com/data-americans-dont-talk-about-money-with-friends-2021-6.

Maher, M, 'Childhood money habits: 8 common ways your parents chapped your fiscal behavior', *iGrad*, 27 April 2021, igrad.com/articles/childhood-money-habits-learned-from-parents.

Merrill, 'The financial journey of modern parenting: Joy, complexity and sacrifice', *Life Stage Series: Parenting*, Bank of America Corporation, 2020, mlaem.fs.ml.com/content/dam/ml/registration/ml_parentstudybrochure.pdf.

Mischel, W, Ebbesen, EB & Zeiss, AR, 'Cognitive and attentional mechanisms in delay of gratification', *Journal of Personality and Social Psychology*, vol. 21, no. 2, 1972, pp. 204–218.

Naragon-Gainey, K, 'How financial stress can affect your mental health and 5 things that can help', *The University of Western Australia*, 17 March 2023, uwa.edu.au/news/Article/2023/March/How-financial-stress-can-affect-your-mental-health-and-5-things-that-can-help.

Newstead, K, 'Aspects of children's mathematics anxiety', *Educational Studies in Mathematics*, vol. 36, 1998, pp. 53–71.

Pape, S, 'It's time to kick the banks out of schools, and teach kids real money skills', *change.org*, 13 June 2021, change.org/p/governments-around-australia-it-s-time-to-kick-the-banks-out-of-schools-and-teach-kids-real-money-skills.

Pattanayak, B, 'In gold we trust: India's household gold reserves valued at over 40% of GDP', *Financial Express*, 20 May 2019, financialexpress.com/market/commodities/shining-bright-indias-household-gold-reserves-touches-25k-tonne-over-40-of-gdp/1583058/.

Quill Group, 'Why don't we want to talk about money', *Quill*, accessed 9 August 2023, quillgroup.com.au/blog/dont-want-talk-money/.

Ross, E & Marshman, M, 'Aussie kids' financial knowledge is on the decline. The proposed national curriculum has downgraded it even further', *The Conversation*, 7 July 2021, theconversation.com/aussie-kids-financial-knowledge-is-on-the-decline-the-proposed-national-curriculum-has-downgraded-it-even-further-163110.

Sawatzki, CM & Sullivan, PA, 'Teachers' perceptions of financial literacy and the implications for professional learning', *Australian Journal of Teacher Education*, vol. 42, no. 5, 2017, pp. 51-65.

Schmidt, T, 'Cash payments more popular in Germany than in other countries', *Research Brief*, Deutsche Bundesbank, February 2016, bundesbank.de/resource/blob/765692/6011d9fb5b2067e4ce8e5559c0d5286c/mL/2016-01-research-brief-data.pdf.

Shoda, Y & Mischel, W, 'Predicting adolescent cognitive and self-regulatory competencies from preschool delay of gratification: Identifying diagnostic conditions', *Developmental Psychology*, vol. 26, no. 6, 1990, pp. 978–986.

Spriggy, 'The pocket money app that helps kids get money smart', accessed 9 August 2023, spriggy.com.au.

Weldon, PR, 'Out-of-field teaching in Australian secondary schools', *Policy Insights*, no. 6, Australian Council for Educational Research, 2016, research.acer.edu.au/policyinsights/6/.

Whitebread, D & Bingham, S, *Habit Formation and Learning in Young Children*, The Money Advice Service, May 2013, mascdn.azureedge.net/cms/the-money-advice-service-habit-formation-and-learning-in-young-children-may2013.pdf.

Wilkins, R, Vera-Toscano, E, Botha, F, Wooden, M & Trinh, T-A, *The Household, Income and Labour Dynamics in Australia Survey: Selected Findings from Waves 1 to 20: The 17th Annual Statistical Report of the HILDA Survey*, The Melbourne Institute, 2022, melbourneinstitute. unimelb.edu.au/__data/assets/pdf_file/0011/4382057/HILDA_Statistical_ Report_2022.pdf.

Wong, L, 'Switching banks is less painful than you think', *ABC Everyday*, 27 August 2018, abc.net.au/everyday/how-to-switch-banks/10007610.

Worthman, CM, Tomlinson, M & Rotheram-Borus, MJ, 'When can parents most influence their child's development? Expert knowledge and perceived local realities', *Social Science & Medicine*, vol. 154, 2016, pp. 62–69.

Zhang, L, Brooks, R, Ding, d, Ding, H, He, H, Lu, J & Mano, R, 'China's high savings: Drivers, prospects, and policies', *IMF Working Paper*, International Monetary Fund, December 2018, imf.org/-/media/Files/ Publications/WP/2018/wp18277.ashx.

Be better with business books

MAJOR STREET

We hope you enjoy reading this book. We'd love you to post a review on social media or your favourite bookseller site. Please include the hashtag #majorstreetpublishing.

Major Street Publishing specialises in business, leadership, personal finance and motivational non-fiction books. If you'd like to receive regular updates about new Major Street books, email info@majorstreet.com.au and ask to be added to our mailing list.

Visit majorstreet.com.au to find out more about our books (print, audio and ebooks) and authors, read reviews and find links to our Your Next Read podcast.

We'd love you to follow us on social media.

in linkedin.com/company/major-street-publishing

f facebook.com/MajorStreetPublishing

instagram.com/majorstreetpublishing

@MajorStreetPub

Milton Keynes UK
Ingram Content Group UK Ltd.
UKHW011427080724
445334UK00032B/668